Reproductive Rights

Other books in the Issues on Trial series:

Reproductive Rights

William Dudley, Book Editor

GREENHAVEN PRESS

An imprint of Thomson Gale, a part of The Thomson Corporation

Detroit • New York • San Francisco • San Diego • New Haven, Conn.
Waterville, Maine • London • Munich

LIBRARY OF CONGRESS CATALOGING-IN-PUBLICATION DATA

Reproductive rights / William Dudley, book editor.
    p. cm. -- (Issues on Trial)
    Includes bibliographical references and index.
    ISBN 0-7377-2511-7 (lib. : alk. paper)
    1. Human reproduction--Law and legislation--United States. 2. Abortion--Law and legislation--United States. 3. Birth control--Law and legislation--United States. I. Dudley, William, 1964– II. Series.
    KF3760.A75R47 2006
    344.7304V8--dc22

                                                                    2005054268

Printed in the United States of America
10 9 8 7 6 5 4 3 2 1

Contents

Chapter 2: Legalizing Contraception

cial policy and argues that the *Griswold* decision helped pave the way for legalizing abortion eight years later.

Chapter 3: Legalizing Abortion

Foreword

The U.S. courts have long served as a battleground for the most highly charged and contentious issues of the time. Divisive matters are often brought into the legal system by activists who feel strongly for their cause and demand an official resolution. Indeed, subjects that give rise to intense emotions or involve closely held religious or moral beliefs lay at the heart of the most polemical court rulings in history. One such case was *Brown v. Board of Education* (1954), which ended racial segregation in schools. Prior to *Brown*, the courts had held that blacks could be forced to use separate facilities as long as these facilities were equal to that of whites.

For years many groups had opposed segregation based on religious, moral, and legal grounds. Educators produced heartfelt testimony that segregated schooling greatly disadvantaged black children. They noted that in comparison to whites, blacks received a substandard education in deplorable conditions. Religious leaders such as Martin Luther King Jr. preached that the harsh treatment of blacks was immoral and unjust. Many involved in civil rights law, such as Thurgood Marshall, called for equal protection of all people under the law, as their study of the Constitution had indicated that segregation was illegal and un-American. Whatever their motivation for ending the practice, and despite the threats they received from segregationists, these ardent activists remained unwavering in their cause.

Those fighting against the integration of schools were mainly white southerners who did not believe that whites and blacks should intermingle. Blacks were subordinate to whites, they maintained, and society had to resist any attempt to break down strict color lines. Some white southerners charged that segregated schooling was *not* hindering blacks' education. For example, Virginia attorney general J. Lindsay Almond asserted, "With the help and the sympathy and the love and respect of the white people of the South, the colored man has risen under that educational process to a place of eminence and respect throughout the nation. It has served him well." So when the Supreme Court ruled against the segregationists in *Brown*, the South responded with vociferous cries of protest. Even government leaders criticized the decision. The governor of Arkansas, Orval Faubus, stated that he would not "be a party to any attempt to force acceptance of change to which the people are so overwhelmingly opposed." Indeed, resistance to integration was so great that when black students arrived at the formerly all-white Central High School in Arkansas, federal troops had to be dispatched to quell a threatening mob of protesters.

Nevertheless, the *Brown* decision was enforced and the South integrated its schools. In this instance, the Court, while not settling the issue to everyone's satisfaction, functioned as an instrument of progress by forcing a major social change. Historian David Halberstam observes that the *Brown* ruling "deprived segregationist practices of their moral legitimacy.... It was therefore perhaps the single most important moment of the decade, the moment that separated the old order from the new and helped create the tumultuous era just arriving." Considered one of the most important victories for civil rights, *Brown* paved the way for challenges to racial segregation in many areas, including on public buses and in restaurants.

In examining *Brown*, it becomes apparent that the courts play an influential role—and face an arduous challenge—in shaping the debate over emotionally charged social issues. Judges must balance competing interests, keeping in mind the high stakes and intense emotions on both sides. As exemplified by *Brown*, judicial decisions often upset the status quo and initiate significant changes in society. Greenhaven Press's Issues on Trial series captures the controversy surrounding influential court rulings and explores the social ramifications of such decisions from varying perspectives. Each anthology highlights one social issue—such as the death penalty, students' rights, or wartime civil liberties. Each volume then focuses on key historical and contemporary court cases that helped mold the issue as we know it today. The books include a compendium of primary sources—court rulings, dissents, and immediate reactions to the rulings—as well as secondary sources from experts in the field, people involved in the cases, legal analysts, and other commentators opining on the implications and legacy of the chosen cases. An annotated table of contents, an in-depth introduction, and prefaces that overview each case all provide context as readers delve into the topic at hand. To help students fully probe the subject, each volume contains book and periodical bibliographies, a comprehensive index, and a list of organizations to contact. With these features, the Issues on Trial series offers a well-rounded perspective on the courts' role in framing society's thorniest, most impassioned debates.

Introduction

For many people, the term *reproductive rights* signifies the issue of abortion and the ongoing debate in America over whether women should have the legal right to choose to terminate a pregnancy. The abortion controversy is indeed central to discussions about reproduction rights. But while abortion may have attracted the most attention from the media, the legal profession, and the public, "reproductive rights" also refers to a constellation of decisions people make regarding their sexual activity and procreation. These decisions—perhaps the most personal and private choices people make—touch on such issues as contraception, sex education, sterilization laws, surrogate parenting, and in-vitro fertilization, in addition to abortion. Whether or not society has the power to regulate such personal decisions has been an ongoing controversy in American history, especially in recent decades—a controversy that has in large part played out in the courts.

The United States has a long history of laws affecting reproduction. Connecticut in 1821 was the first state to pass a law criminalizing abortion. (Prior to that, abortion was governed by British common law, which held that the practice was legal before "quickening"—the feeling of fetal movement by the mother, usually sometime after four months into the pregnancy.) By the end of the nineteenth century all states had passed some sort of abortion legislation that either banned abortion entirely or permitted only therapeutic abortions done to save the life of the mother. In addition to abortion laws, many states passed laws banning the sale or use of barrier contraceptive devices such as the diaphragm and condom. An 1873 federal statute (known as the Comstock law) defined information about birth control as obscene and made it a federal crime to import or send such information through the mail. In the early twentieth century many states also passed

A Planned Parenthood employee holds a poster that was displayed on New York's buses and subways in the 1960s. The Supreme Court ruled in 1965 that laws banning contraception are unconstitutional. © Hulton-Deutsch Collection/CORBIS

laws providing for the involuntary sterilization of criminals and people deemed by medical experts to have limited intelligence.

The motivations for these laws restricting reproductive freedom were varied. Some were spurred by religious teachings on the immorality of abortion and contraception. For example, the Roman Catholic Church opposed contraception and proclaimed in 1895 that abortion is never justifiable because it kills the fetus; these religious pronouncements were especially influential in states and cities with large Catholic populations. Some lawmakers feared for the safety of women obtaining abortions, or considered public discussions of sex and contraception to be indecent. Doctors with the American Medical Association, established in 1847, pushed for abortion legislation to professionalize the medical field and make abortion a procedure that midwives and others without medical licenses could not perform. Worries about social and demographic trends in the United States also played a role; some lawmakers believed that white middle- and upper-class women should be encouraged to have many children (and thus discouraged from seeking birth control and/or abortion) to prevent the members of these classes from being outnumbered by children of "undesirable" groups such as immigrants and people of color. Similar concerns also lay behind some of the state sterilization laws and fertility control measures that in practice affected members of these groups. But while those who made laws governing reproductive decisions may have had varying goals and social visions, they shared a common notion that society had the right to regulate a person's reproductive decisions—a right greater than any individual right of "choice" in these matters.

In the twentieth century, most of these laws against contraception and abortion, as well as laws legitimizing involuntary sterilization, were overturned or discarded. Some laws were overturned as the result of political and legal action as activists were able to persuade individual state legislatures to repeal or liberalize laws against abortion and contraception. In other places such laws remained on the books while being loosely or selectively enforced. But some of the most important victories of reproductive rights activists occurred in court cases in which they challenged the fairness and constitutionality of laws governing reproductive decisions.

The movement for the legal recognition of reproductive rights had to overcome one major stumbling block: Such rights, including abortion, contraception, and the right to have or not have children, are nowhere mentioned in the U.S. Constitution or its amendments. These rights may arguably fall under a general "right to privacy"—but that right also is not mentioned in the U.S. Constitution. One legal solution to this quandary, according to reproductive rights supporters, could be found in the Fourteenth Amendment to the Constitution. The amendment, ratified in 1868, includes the provision, "Nor shall any state deprive any person of life, liberty, or property without due process of law." The U.S. Supreme Court has in some cases cited the due process clause as a basis for overturning state laws that restricted certain basic freedoms the Court deemed to be fundamental to liberty.

In recent decades, the Supreme Court has ruled that such fundamental freedoms included decisions pertaining to reproduction. Thus, in *Skinner v. Oklahoma* (1942), the Supreme Court mentioned the "right to procreate" while invalidating a state law providing for the sterilization of convicted criminals. In the 1965 case of *Griswold v. Connecticut,* the Court overturned a state law forbidding married couples to use contraception. The justices held that the Fourteenth Amendment, in combination with other guarantees in the Bill of Rights, created a fundamental right to privacy, and that this right included the right of married couples to use contraception. In *Eisenstadt v. Baird* (1972), the Court extended the right to use contraception to individuals. In the 1973 case of *Roe v. Wade,* the Court decided that a woman's decision to terminate her pregnancy could also be protected under the right to privacy. However, it did not make the right to abortion absolute, arguing that the state had interests in protecting fetal life in the later stages of pregnancy. The Supreme Court has revisited the abortion issue numerous times since 1973 as federal and state legislatures have continued to pass laws designed to discourage abortion; the Court has upheld some restrictions and overturned others. In the 1992 case of *Planned Parenthood v. Casey,* the Court upheld some regulations, including mandatory waiting periods and parental involvement in a minor's abortion decision, but also reaffirmed a woman's constitutional right to choose abortion free of any "substantial obstacle."

Pro-life and pro-choice activists confront each other during a 2005 demonstration in Washington, D.C. The 1973 Roe v. Wade *ruling is still debated by legal and political groups.* © Micah Walter/Reuters/CORBIS

These decisions—*Roe* especially—have been controversial. Whether or not the Supreme Court acted properly in defining these reproductive rights as constitutional is a question still being debated in legal and political circles. Dissenting Supreme Court justices argued that their colleagues were creating rights not to be found in the text of the Constitution. Similar arguments continue to be made to this day by critics who contend that abortion and other reproductive rights matters should not be dictated by the Supreme Court or any court of law but instead worked out through the legislative branch of government and the political process.

Besides the ongoing controversy over how the Supreme Court should interpret the Constitution, and the balancing of individual freedom versus social control, legal cases involving reproductive rights also often involve a balancing of concerns between different parties in the reproductive process. Abortion opponents argue that unborn children should have constitutional rights. Abortion rights proponents contend that the right of women to control their own bodies should be paramount over any "fetal rights." The role of fathers, and what rights they may have in the abortion decision and other circumstances, has also been the subject of legal battles, especially in cases involving assisted reproductive technology.

The controversy over how much control an individual should have over his or her reproductive decisions remains far from settled. This anthology examines four significant legal cases that have affected the state of reproductive rights in the United States: *Buck v. Bell* (1927), *Griswold v. Connecticut* (1965), *Roe v. Wade* (1973), and *A.Z. v. B.Z.* (2000). The selected readings illustrate how abortion and other reproductive rights issues have become—and continue to be—an ongoing source of political and legal disputes.

CHAPTER 1

Upholding Involuntary Sterilization Laws

Case Overview

Buck v. Bell (1927)

In the 1927 case of *Buck v. Bell,* the U.S. Supreme Court upheld a Virginia law that authorized the state to sterilize people judged by experts to be mentally or physically defective. The case legitimized involuntary sterilization laws and resulted in the sterilization of Carrie Buck, a young woman chosen by authorities to be the first test case of the Virginia law. It also provided validation for supporters of eugenics—the theory that problems such as crime, disease, immorality, and low intelligence be solved by improving the human race through selective breeding and by preventing "inferior" individuals from reproducing.

The law under which Buck was eventually sterilized was a Virginia statute enacted in 1924. The primary author of the law, Aubrey Strobe, was both a state legislator and the chief administrator of the Virginia State Colony for Epileptics and Feeble-Minded—the institution to which both Carrie Buck and her mother, Emma, had been committed. Strobe based his law on a model sterilization act drafted by Harry H. Laughlin, a leading advocate of eugenics who contended that compulsory sterilization laws were essential to protect "the racial health—physical, mental, and spiritual—of future generations."

Virginia was not the first state to enact such legislation. In 1907 Indiana was the first to pass a law for the "prevention of the procreation of confirmed criminals, idiots, imbeciles, and racists." Other states had followed suit. But many of these laws were challenged legally, and sterilizations were seldom carried out. An Indiana state court deemed that state's sterilization law unconstitutional in 1921, for example. Strobe, Laughlin, and others wanted to establish the legality and constitutionality of Virginia's legislation; they chose Carrie Buck, whose mother and newborn daughter had also been pronounced feebleminded by authorities, as their test case.

The case was first argued in late 1924 before a circuit court judge. Witnesses called by the state of Virginia testified about Carrie's character and mental state as well as the mental capacity of other members of her family. Some historians have argued that attorneys representing Buck did not mount a vigorous case and may have gone so far as to collude with the state lawyers. Edwin Black, author of *War Against the Weak*, argued in a 2003 issue of *American Lawyer* that "attorneys representing both the commonwealth of Virginia and Carrie Buck colluded to create the appearance of an independent adversarial lawsuit" and that "Buck, her mother, and her young daughter were all unjustly classified as 'feebleminded.'"

Judge Bennett Gordon ruled in February 1925 to uphold Virginia's law and carry out Carrie Buck's sterilization. His ruling was upheld by the Virginia Court of Appeals and then taken up by the U.S. Supreme Court. Justice Oliver Wendell Holmes delivered the Supreme Court's decision on May 2, 1927, writing for an 8-1 majority in affirming the right of states to sterilize some individuals to benefit the public welfare. The only holdout, associate justice Pierce Butler, did not write a dissenting opinion. Carrie Buck was sterilized on October 19, 1927.

| *"Three generations of imbeciles
| are enough."*

The Court's Decision: Society Has the Right to Sterilize the Mentally Unfit

Oliver Wendell Holmes

Oliver Wendell Holmes, the son of a prominent American writer, was nominated to the Supreme Court by President Theodore Roosevelt in 1902. Holmes had already attained distinction as a Civil War veteran, legal scholar, and Massachusetts state judge. He served as an associate justice for almost thirty years. Holmes wrote and delivered the 8-1 majority opinion in the 1927 case Buck v. Bell, *which validated the right of the state of Virginia to sterilize Carrie Buck, an inmate at a mental health institution. Holmes argues that Buck's constitutional right to due process was adequately protected by the legal procedures and hearings provided by the Virginia law authorizing sterilization of those deemed unfit to reproduce. Holmes also contends that Buck's individual right to have children must be balanced against society's need to protect the social good by preventing "imbeciles" from passing on their traits to their offspring. The* Buck v. Bell *case encouraged other states to follow Virginia's example and enact involuntary sterilization laws.*

This is a writ of error to review a judgment of the Supreme Court of Appeals of the State of Virginia, affirming a judgment of the Circuit Court of Amherst County, by which the defendant in error, the superintendent of the State Colony for Epileptics and Feeble Minded, was ordered to perform the operation of salpingectomy [severing the fallopian tubes] upon Carrie Buck, the plaintiff in error, for the purpose of

Oliver Wendell Holmes, majority opinion, *Buck v. Bell,* 274 U.S. 200, 1927.

making her sterile. The case comes here upon the contention that the statute authorizing the judgment is void under the Fourteenth Amendment as denying to the plaintiff in error due process of law and the equal protection of the laws.

Buck Has Received Due Process

Carrie Buck is a feeble-minded white woman who was committed to the State Colony above mentioned in due form. She is the daughter of a feeble-minded mother in the same institution, and the mother of an illegitimate feeble-minded child. She was eighteen years old at the time of the trial of her case in the Circuit Court in the latter part of 1924. An Act of Virginia approved March 20, 1924 recites that the health of the patient and the welfare of society may be promoted in certain cases by the sterilization of mental defectives, under careful safeguard, etc.; that the sterilization may be effected in males by vasectomy and in females by salpingectomy, without serious pain or substantial danger to life; that the Commonwealth is supporting in various institutions many defective persons who if now discharged would become a menace but if incapable of procreating might be discharged with safety and become self-supporting with benefit to themselves and to society; and that experience has shown that heredity plays an important part in the transmission of insanity, imbecility, etc. The statute then enacts that whenever the superintendent of certain institutions including the abovenamed State Colony shall be of opinion that it is for the best interest of the patients and of society that an inmate under his care should be sexually sterilized, he may have the operation performed upon any patient afflicted with hereditary forms of insanity, imbecility, etc., on complying with the very careful provisions by which the act protects the patients from possible abuse.

The superintendent first presents a petition to the special board of directors of his hospital or colony, stating the facts and the grounds for his opinion, verified by affidavit. Notice

Justice Oliver Wendell Holmes wrote the majority opinion in the 1927 case Buck v. Bell, *which authorized the state of Virginia to sterilize people deemed mentally or physically defective.* Collection of the Supreme Court of the United States

of the petition and of the time and place of the hearing in the institution is to be served upon the inmate, and also upon his guardian, and if there is no guardian the superintendent is to apply to the Circuit Court of the County to appoint one. If the inmate is a minor, notice also is to be given to his parents, if any, with a copy of the petition. The board is to see to it that the inmate may attend the hearings if desired by him or his guardian. The evidence is all to be reduced to writing, and after the board has made its order for or against the operation, the superintendent, or the inmate, or his guardian, may appeal to the Circuit Court of the County. The Circuit Court may consider the record of the board and the evidence before it and such other admissible evidence as may be offered, and may affirm, revise, or reverse the order of the board and enter such order as it deems just. Finally any party may apply to the

Supreme Court of Appeals, which, if it grants the appeal, is to hear the case upon the record of the trial in the Circuit Court and may enter such order as it thinks the Circuit Court should have entered. There can be no doubt that so far as procedure is concerned the rights of the patient are most carefully considered, and as every step in this case was taken in scrupulous compliance with the statute and after months of observation, there is no doubt that in that respect the plaintiff in error has had due process at law.

The Public Welfare

The attack is not upon the procedure but upon the substantive law. It seems to be contended that in no circumstances could such an order be justified. It certainly is contended that the order cannot be justified upon the existing grounds. The judgment finds the facts that have been recited and that Carrie Buck "is the probable potential parent of socially inadequate offspring, likewise afflicted, that she may be sexually sterilized without detriment to her general health and that her welfare and that of society will be promoted by her sterilization," and thereupon makes the order. In view of the general declarations of the Legislature and the specific findings of the Court obviously we cannot say as matter of law that the grounds do not exist, and if they exist they justify the result. We have seen more than once that the public welfare may call upon the best citizens for their lives. It would be strange if it could not call upon those who already sap the strength of the State for these lesser sacrifices, often not felt to be such by those concerned, in order to prevent our being swamped with incompetence. It is better for all the world, if instead of waiting to execute degenerate offspring for crime, or to let them starve for their imbecility, society can prevent those who are manifestly unfit from continuing their kind. The principle that sustains compulsory vaccination is broad enough to cover cutting the Fallopian tubes. Three generations of imbeciles are enough. But, it is said, however it might be if this reasoning were applied generally, it fails when it is confined to the small number who are in the institutions named and is not applied to the multitudes outside. It is the usual last resort of constitutional arguments to point out shortcomings of this sort. But the answer is that the law does all that is needed when it does all that it can, indicates a policy, applies it to all within the lines, and seeks to bring within the lines all similarly situated so far and so fast as its means allow. Of course so far as the operations enable those who otherwise must be kept confined to be returned to the world, and thus open the asylum to others, the equality aimed at will be more nearly reached.

"The welfare of society may be promoted in certain cases by the sterilization of mental defectives under careful safeguard."

Public Reaction to *Buck v. Bell*

Literary Digest

The Supreme Court's decision in Buck v. Bell *(1927) to validate involuntary sterilization laws was generally well received by opinion leaders and the public. The decision was made at a time when many were worried that people with defective physical and mental traits were having too many children and thus harming the country. The following selection, taken from an article in the journal* Literary Digest, *surveys what newspaper editorials had to say about* Buck v. Bell. *Most of the newspaper editors favored the decision and the Virginia state law in question and argued that sterilization was a worthwhile method of ridding the United States of undesirables.*

Nothing has called forth more acrimonious debate than the subject of State sterilization in the case of incurable mental defectives, in the opinion of the New York *Evening World*. There are now [in 1927] perhaps fifteen States, we are told, which authorize this operation to prevent the birth of children to feeble-minded parents, in the interest of the welfare of society and the health of the patient. But until May 2 the Supreme Court of the United States had not passed on the question. On that date, Associate Justice Oliver Wendell Holmes, son of a physician as well as a poet, upheld the broad right of society to protect itself against the perpetuation of the imbecile and hopelessly unfit. Specifically, the Supreme

Literary Digest, "To Halt the Imbecile's Perilous Line," vol. XCIII, May 21, 1927.

Court upheld a Virginia law providing for the sterilization of mental defectives. Only Associate Justice [Pierce] Butler dissented from the majority ruling, and he filed no written opinion. "This should end the controversy over the country's sterilization laws," believes the New Orleans *Times-Picayune.*

Common Sense vs. Sentimentality

The Virginia law, it seems, had been pronounced valid by the State Supreme Court, but was carried to the highest tribunal on the ground that the plaintiff had been deprived, contrary to the Fourteenth Amendment, of due process and protection of law. The importance of the Supreme Court decision, observes the New York *World,* "lies in the fact that such legislation has already gone further in the United States than any other part of the world." According to the Birmingham *Age-Herald:*

> Sociologists have long urged the sterilization of the feeble-minded. Now that the Supreme Court has declared constitutional the Virginia statute providing for such treatment, other States can be expected to follow suit, with the result that a great menace, growing rapidly so long as reproduction was possible, will now be confined, and as time goes on reduced to a minimum, by scientific means.
>
> Sentimentality and a false conception of individual right have hitherto prevented the courageous dealing with this problem of the feeble-minded. We have known that mental defect is hereditary and incurable; that 50 per cent. of reformatory inmates and almost as many adult prisoners are mentally defective; that investigations have shown more than half the number of prostitutes, four-fifths of truants, and one-half of paupers to be feeble-minded. The decision of the Supreme Court is to be hailed by all thoughtful persons as giving impetus to a candid facing and a fearless solution of the problem.
>
> This is not a matter of yielding to [Friedrich] Nietzsche's doctrine of the superman, weeding out the weak in order

that the strong may be stronger. This is merely common sense used in the interest of self-protection. If the nation is to guard itself against mental taint, with its incalculable consequences of crime and debility, it must surely employ the simple measure of sterilization.

The woman whose case came before the Supreme Court, we are told, is twenty-one years old, feeble-minded, and an inmate of the Virginia State Colony for Feeble-Minded. She is unmarried, but is the mother of a feeble-minded child. Her mother, also feeble-minded, is likewise an inmate of the Colony. "Three generations of imbeciles are enough," said Justice Holmes, in his ruling.

Health and Welfare

The Virginia Act, say Washington dispatches, recites that the health of the patient and the welfare of society may be promoted in certain cases by the sterilization of mental defectives under careful safeguard; that the sterilization may be effected without serious pain or substantial danger to life; that the Commonwealth is supporting in various institutions many defectives who, if now discharged, would become a menace, but who if sterilized might be discharged with benefit to themselves and society.

In his decision, Justice Holmes maintains that society has the right to require that the mentally weak shall not bring children into the world who will themselves be feeble-minded and a burden to the State, either through crime or dependence. It is a curious fact, notes the Brooklyn *Eagle,* that the father of Justice Holmes, a physician, pointed out that genius—or stupidity—may jump three or four generations, and reappear in offspring. Thus the child of a feeble-minded person might inherit genius from a great-great-grandfather. "But," *The Eagle* goes on, "this chance, in the opinion of Justice Holmes, apparently is so slender as to be negligible in the broad view of human society." At any rate, the Associate Justice, in handing down his decision. said, in part:

> The provisions of the Virginia Act include requirements for public hearings, reduction of all evidence to writing, appeal to the Circuit Court of the county, and finally appeal to the highest court of the State. There can be no doubt that so far as procedure is concerned, the rights of the patients are most carefully considered, and as every step in this case was taken in scrupulous compliance with the statute and after months of observation, there is no doubt that in that respect the plaintiff in error has had due process of law.

> It is better for all the world, if, instead of waiting to execute degenerate offspring for crime, society can prevent those who are manifestly unfit from continuing their kind.

Protecting America's Stock

According to the "World Almanac," the number of feeble-minded persons in institutions in the United States is 39.3 per 100,000 of total population, as against 22.5 in 1910. "The stock of the entire country is being constantly poisoned and vitiated," declares *The Twin City Sentinel,* of Winston-Salem. "With a reasonably rigid enforcement of sterilization laws throughout the land," adds this North Carolina daily, "this nation could be pretty well rid of the worst types of mental weaklings within the next two generations."

There is, however, danger that these sterilization laws will be abused unless they are carefully safeguarded, points out the Philadelphia *Bulletin.* In the opinion of the Hartford *Times:*

> The difficulty is that information upon the transmitting of characteristics is so slight and the variety of opinion so great, that the laying down of the general principle that the State may decide arbitrarily who shall be allowed to have children and who shall be prevented from doing so seems dangerous.

> "The campaign for forced eugenic steril-
> ization in America reached its ... height
> of respectability ... in the case of Buck v.
> Bell."

Buck v. Bell Was Based on
False Assertions of Fact

Stephen Jay Gould

*Stephen Jay Gould was an evolutionary biologist and prolific sci-
ence writer who died in 2002. The following selection, taken
from one of his three hundred columns for* Natural History
magazine, examines the facts behind the 1927 case of Buck v.
Bell, *in which the U.S. Supreme Court validated a Virginia state
law that provided for the involuntary sterilization of people
deemed unfit. Gould notes that the rationale behind sterilizing
Carrie Buck—the appellant in the case—was that she, her
mother, and her six-month-old daughter were all deemed "feeble-
minded." Because the condition was deemed inheritable, the
state of Virginia contended that Buck needed to be sterilized in
order to prevent the birth of additional "feeble-minded" children. Gould writes that historical investigations decades later revealed that Carrie Buck was placed into a mental health institution to cover up a scandalous pregnancy, that she was not in fact
mentally deficient, and that school records revealed that her
daughter was also mentally sound.*

The Lord really put it on the line in his preface to that prototype of all prescription, the Ten Commandements:

> for I, the Lord thy God, am a jealous God, visiting the iniq-
> uity of the fathers upon the children unto the third and
> fourth generation of them that hate me (Exod. 20:5).

Stephen Jay Gould, "Carrie Buck's Daughter," *Natural History,* July 1984. Copyright ©
1984 by the American Museum of Natural History. Reproduced by permission of the
author's estate.

The terror of this statement lies in its patent unfairness—its promise to punish guiltless offspring for the misdeeds of their distant forebears.

A different form of guilt by genealogical association attempts to remove this stigma of injustice by denying a cherished premise of Western thought—human free will. If offspring are tainted not simply by the deeds of their parents but by a material form of evil transferred directly by biological inheritance, "the iniquity of the fathers" becomes a signal or warning for probable misbehavior of their sons. Thus Plato, while denying that children should suffer directly for the crimes of their parents, nonetheless defended the banishment of a man whose father, grandfather, and great-grandfather had all been condemned to death.

It is, perhaps, merely coincidental that both Jehovah and Plato chose three generations as their criterion for establishing different forms of guilt by association. Yet we have a strong folk, or vernacular, tradition for viewing triple occurrences as minimal evidence of regularity. We are told that bad things come in threes. Two may be an accidental association; three is a pattern. Perhaps, then, we should not wonder that our own century's most famous pronouncement of blood guilt employed the same criterion—Oliver Wendell Holmes's defense of compulsory sterilization in Virginia (Supreme Court decision of 1927 in *Buck v. Bell:* "three generations of imbeciles are enough."

Restrictions upon immigration, with national quotas set to discriminate against those deemed mentally unfit by early versions of IQ testing, marked the greatest triumph of the American eugenics movement—the flawed hereditarian doctrine, so popular earlier in our century and by no means extinct today (see my column on Singapore's "great marriage debate," May 1984), that attempted to "improve" our human stock by preventing the propagation of those deemed biologically unfit and encouraging procreation among the supposedly worthy.

But the movement to enact and enforce laws for compulsory "eugenic" sterilization had an impact and success scarcely less pronounced. If we could debar the shiftless and the stupid from our shores, we might also prevent the propagation of those similarly afflicted but already here.

The movement for compulsory sterilization began in earnest during the 1890s, abetted by two major factors—the rise of eugenics as an influential political movement and the perfection of safe and simple operations (vasectomy for men and salpingectomy, the cutting and tying of Fallopian tubes, for women) to replace castration and other obvious mutilation. Indiana passed the first sterilization act based on eugenic principles in 1907 (a few states had previously mandated castration as a punitive measure for certain sexual crimes, although such laws were rarely enforced and usually overturned by judicial review). Like so many others to follow, it provided for sterilization of afflicted people residing in the state's "care," either as inmates of mental hospitals and homes for the feebleminded or as inhabitants of prisons. Sterilization could be imposed upon those judged insane, idiotic, imbecilic, or moronic, and upon convicted rapists or criminals when recommended by a board of experts.

By the 1930s, more than thirty states had passed similar laws, often with an expanded list of so-called hereditary defects, including alcoholism and drug addiction in some states, and even blindness and deafness in others. It must be said that these laws were continually challenged and rarely enforced in most states; only California and Virginia applied them zealously. By January 1935, some 20,000 forced "eugenic" sterilizations had been performed in the United States, nearly half in California.

Harry Laughlin's Crusade

No organization crusaded more vociferously and successfully for these laws than the Eugenics Record Office, the semiofficial arm and repository of data for the eugenics movement in America. Harry Laughlin, superintendent of the Eugenics Record Office, dedicated most of his career to a tireless campaign of writing and lobbying for eugenic sterilization. He hoped, thereby, to eliminate in two generations the genes of what he called the "submerged tenth"—"the most worthless one-tenth of our present population." He proposed a "model sterilization law" in 1922, designed

> to prevent the procreation of persons socially inadequate from defective inheritance, by authorizing and providing for eugenical sterilization of certain potential parents carrying degenerate hereditary qualities.

This model bill became the prototype for most laws passed in America, although few states cast their net as widely as Laughlin advised. (Laughlin's categories encompassed "blind, including those with seriously impaired vision; deaf, including those with seriously impaired hearing; and dependent, including orphans, ne'er-do-wells, the homeless, tramps, and paupers.") Laughlin's suggestions were better heeded in Nazi Germany, where his model act served as a basis for [German eugenics laws] leading by the eve of World War II to the sterilization of some 375,000 people, most for "congenital feeble-mindedness," but including nearly 4,000 for blindness and deafness.

The campaign for forced eugenic sterilization in America reached its climax and height of respectability in 1927, when the Supreme Court, by an 8-1 vote, upheld the Virginia sterilization bill in the case of *Buck v. Bell*. Oliver Wendell Holmes, then in his mid-eighties and the most celebrated jurist in America, wrote the majority opinion with his customary verve and power of style. It included the notorious paragraph, with its chilling tag line, cited ever since as the quintessential statement of eugenic principles. Remembering with pride his own distant experiences as an infantryman in the Civil War, Holmes wrote:

We have seen more than once that the public welfare may call upon the best citizens for their lives. It would be strange if it could not call upon those who already sap the strength of the state for these lesser sacrifices.... It is better for all the world, if instead of waiting to execute degenerate offspring for crime, or to let them starve for their imbecility, society can prevent those who are manifestly unfit from continuing their kind. The principle that sustains compulsory vaccination is broad enough to cover cutting the Fallopian tubes. Three generations of imbeciles are enough.

Who, then, were the famous "three generations of imbeciles," and why should they still compel our interest?

Who Was Carrie Buck?

When the state of Virginia passed its compulsory sterilization law in 1924, Carrie Buck, an eighteen-year-old white woman, was an involuntary resident at the State Colony for Epileptics and Feeble-Minded. As the first person selected for sterilization under the new act, Carrie Buck became the focus for a constitutional challenge launched, in part, by conservative Virginia Christians who held, according to eugenical "modernists," antiquated views about individual preferences and "benevolent" state power. (Simplistic political labels do not apply in this case, and rarely do in general. We usually regard eugenics as a conservative movement and its most vocal critics as members of the left. This alignment has generally held in our own decade. But eugenics, touted in its day as the latest in scientific modernism, attracted many liberals and numbered among its most vociferous critics groups often labeled as reactionary and antiscientific. If any political lesson emerges from these shifting allegiances, we might consider the true inalienability of certain human rights.)

But why was Carrie Buck in the State Colony, and why was she selected? Oliver Wendell Holmes upheld her choice as judicious in the opening lines of his 1927 opinion:

Carrie Buck is a feeble-minded white woman who was committed to the State Colony. . . . She is the daughter of a feeble-minded mother in the same institution, and the mother of an illegitimate feeble-minded child.

In short, inheritance stood as the crucial issue (indeed as the driving force behind all eugenics). For if measured mental deficiency arose from malnourishment, either of body or mind, and not from tainted genes, then how could sterilization be justified? If decent food, upbringing, medical care, and education might make a worthy citizen of Carrie Buck's daughter, how could the State of Virginia justify the severing of Carrie's Fallopian tubes against her will? (Some forms of mental deficiency are passed by inheritance in family line, but most are not—a scarcely surprising conclusion when we consider the thousand shocks that beset fragile humans during their lives, from difficulties in embryonic growth to traumas of birth, malnourishment, rejection, and poverty. In any case, no fair-minded person today would credit Laughlin's social criteria for the identification of hereditary deficiency—ne'er-do-wells, the homeless, tramps, and paupers—although we shall soon see that Carrie Buck was committed on these grounds.)

When Carrie Buck's case emerged as the crucial test of Virginia's law, the chief honchos of eugenics knew that the time had come to put up or shut up on the crucial issue of inheritance. Thus, the Eugenics Record Office sent Arthur H. Estabrook, their crack fieldworker, to Virginia for a "scientific" study of the case. Harry Laughlin himself provided a deposition, and his brief for inheritance was presented at the local trial that affirmed Virginia's law and later worked its way to the Supreme Court as *Buck v. Bell.*

Laughlin's Case

Laughlin made two major points to the court. First, that Carrie Buck and her mother, Emma Buck, were feeble-minded by the Stanford-Binet test of IQ, then in its own infancy. Carrie scored a mental age of nine years, Emma of seven years and eleven months. (These figures ranked them technically as "imbeciles" by definitions of the day, hence Holmes's later choice of words. Imbeciles displayed a mental age of six to nine years; idiots performed worse, morons better, to round out the old nomenclature of mental deficiency.) Second, that most feeblemindedness is inherited, and Carrie Buck surely belonged with this majority. Laughlin reported:

> Generally feeble-mindedness is caused by the inheritance of degenerate qualities; but sometimes it might be caused by environmental factors which are not hereditary. In the case given, the evidence points strongly toward the feeble-mindedness and moral delinquency of Carrie Buck being due, primarily, to inheritance and not to environment.

Carrie Buck's daughter was then, and has always been, the pivotal figure of this painful case. . . . We tend (often at our peril) to regard two as potential accident and three as an established pattern. The supposed imbecility of Emma and Carrie might have been coincidental, but the diagnosis of similar deficiency for Vivian Buck (made by a social worker, as we shall see, when Vivian was but six months old) tipped the balance in Laughlin's favor and led Holmes to declare the Buck lineage inherently corrupt by deficient heredity. Vivian sealed the pattern—three generations of imbeciles are enough. Besides, had Carrie not given illegitimate birth to Vivian, the issue (in both senses) would never have emerged.

Oliver Wendell Holmes viewed his work with pride. The man so renowned for his principle of judicial restraint, who had proclaimed that freedom must not be curtailed without "clear and present danger"—without the equivalent of falsely yelling "fire" in a crowded theater—wrote of his judgment in *Buck v. Bell*: "I felt that I was getting near the first principle of real reform."

New and Disturbing Research

And so the case of *Buck v. Bell* remained for fifty years, a footnote to a moment of American history perhaps best forgotten. And then, in 1980, it reemerged to prick our collective conscience, when Dr. K. Ray Nelson, then director of the Lynchburg Hospital where Carrie Buck was sterilized, researched the records of his institution and discovered that more than 4,000 sterilizations had been performed, the last as late as 1972. He also found Carrie Buck, alive and well near Charlottesville, and her sister Doris, covertly sterilized under the same law (she was told that her operation was for appendicitis), and now, with fierce dignity, dejected and bitter because she had wanted a child more than anything else in her life and had finally, in her old age, learned why she had never conceived.

As scholars and reporters visited Carrie Buck and her sister, what a few experts had known all along became abundantly clear to everyone. Carrie Buck was a woman of obviously normal intelligence. For example, Paul A. Lombardo of the School of Law at the University of Virginia, and a leading scholar of the *Buck v. Bell* case, wrote in a letter to me:

> As for Carrie, when I met her she was reading newspapers daily and joining a more literate friend to assist at regular bouts with the crossword puzzles. She was not a sophisticated woman, and lacked social graces, but mental health professionals who examined her in later life confirmed my impressions that she was neither mentally ill nor retarded.

On what evidence, then, was Carrie Buck consigned to the State Colony for Epileptics and Feeble-Minded on January 23, 1924? I have seen the text of her commitment hearing; it is, to say the least, cursory and contradictory. Beyond the simple and undocumented say-so of her foster parents, and her own brief appearance before a commission of two doctors and a justice of the peace, no evidence was presented. Even the crude and early Stanford-Binet test, so fatally flawed as a measure of innate worth (see my book *The Mismeasure of Man,* although the evidence of Carrie's own case suffices) but at least clothed with the aura of quantitative respectability, had not yet been applied.

A Secret Uncovered

When we understand why Carrie Buck was committed in January 1924, we can finally comprehend the hidden meaning of her case and its message for us today. The silent key, again and as always, is her daughter Vivian, born on March 28, 1924, and then but an evident bump on her belly. Carrie Buck was one of several illegitimate children borne by her mother, Emma. She grew up with foster parents, J.T. and Alice Dobbs, and continued to live with them, helping out with chores around the house. She was apparently raped by a relative of her foster parents, then blamed for her resultant pregnancy. Almost surely, she was (as they used to say) committed to hide her shame (and her rapist's identity), not because enlightened science had just discovered her true mental status. In short, she was sent away to have her baby. Her case never was about mental deficiency; it was always a matter of sexual morality and social deviance. The annals of her trial and hearing reek with the contempt of the well-off and well-bred for poor people of "loose morals." Who really cared whether Vivian was a baby of normal intelligence; she was the illegitimate child of an illegitimate woman. Two generations of bastards are enough. Harry Laughlin began his "family history" of the Bucks by writing: "These people belong to the shiftless, ignorant and worthless class of anti-social whites of the South."

We know little of Emma Buck and her life, but we have no more reason to suspect her than her daughter Carrie of true mental deficiency. Their deviance was social and sexual; the charge of imbecility was a cover-up, Mr. Justice Holmes notwithstanding.

We come then to the crux of the case, Carrie's daughter, Vivian. What evidence was ever adduced for her mental deficiency? This and only this: At the original trial in late 1924, when Vivian Buck was seven months old, a Miss Wilhelm, social worker for the Red Cross, appeared before the court. She began by stating honestly the true reason for Carrie Buck's commitment:

> Mr. Dobbs, who had charge of the girl, had taken her when a small child, had reported to Miss Duke [the temporary secretary of Public Welfare for Albemarle County] that the girl was pregnant and that he wanted to have her committed somewhere—to have her sent to some institution.

Miss Wilhelm then rendered her judgment of Vivian Buck by comparing her with the normal granddaughter of Mrs. Dobbs, born just three days earlier:

> It is difficult to judge probabilities of a child as young as that, but it seems to me not quite a normal baby. In its appearance—I should say that perhaps my knowledge of the mother may prejudice me in that regard, but I saw the child at the same time as Mrs. Dobbs' daughter's baby, which is only three days older than this one, and there is a very decided difference in the development of the babies. That was about two weeks ago. There is a look about it that is not quite normal, but just what it is, I can't tell.

This short testimony, and nothing else, formed all the evidence for the crucial third generation of imbeciles. Cross-examination revealed that neither Vivian nor the Dobbs grandchild could walk or talk, and that "Mrs. Dobbs' daughter's baby is a very responsive baby. When you play with it or try to attract its attention—it is a baby that you can play with. The other baby is not. It seems very apathetic and not responsive." Miss Wilhelm then urged Carrie Buck's sterilization: "I think," she said, "it would at least prevent the propagation of her kind." Several years later, Miss Wilhelm denied that she had ever examined Vivian or deemed the child feebleminded.

Vivian's Intelligence

Unfortunately, Vivian died at age eight of "enteric colitis" (as recorded on her death certificate), an ambiguous diagnosis that could mean many things but may well indicate that she fell victim to one of the preventable childhood diseases of poverty (a grim reminder of the real subject in *Buck v. Bell*). She is therefore mute as a witness in our reassessment of her famous case.

When *Buck v. Bell* resurfaced in 1980, it immediately struck me that Vivian's case was crucial and that evidence for the mental status of a child who died at age eight might best be found in report cards. I have therefore been trying to track down Vivian Buck's school records for the past four years and have finally succeeded. (They were supplied to me by Dr. Paul A. Lombardo, who also sent other documents, including Miss Wilhelm's testimony, and spent several hours answering my questions by mail and Lord knows how much time playing successful detective in re Vivian's school records. I have never met Dr. Lombardo; he did all this work for kindness, collegiality, and love of the game of knowledge, not for expected reward or even requested acknowledgment. In a profession—academics—so often marked by pettiness and silly squabbling over meaningless priorities, this generosity must be recorded and celebrated as a sign of how things can and should be.)

Vivian Buck was adopted by the Dobbs family, who had raised (but later sent away) her mother, Carrie. As Vivian Alice Elaine Dobbs, she attended the Venable Public Elementary School of Charlottesville for four terms, from September 1930 until May 1932, a month before her death. She was a perfectly normal, quite average student, neither particularly outstanding nor much troubled. In those days before grade inflation, when C meant "good, 81–87" (as defined on her report card) rather than barely scraping by, Vivian Dobbs received A's and B's for deportment and C's for all academic subjects but mathematics (which was always difficult for her, and where she scored D) during her first term in Grade 1A, from September 1930 to January 1931. She improved during her second term in 1B, meriting an A in deportment, C in mathematics, and B in all other academic subjects; she was on the honor roll in April 1931. Promoted to 2A, she had trouble during the fall term of 1931, failing mathematics and spelling but receiving A in deportment, B in reading, and C in writing and English. She was "retained in 2A" for the next term—or "left back" as we used to say, and scarcely a sign of imbecility as I remember all my buddies who suffered a similar fate. In any case, she again did well in her final term, with B in deportment, reading, and spelling, and C in writing, English, and mathematics during her last month in school. This offspring of "lewd and immoral" women excelled in deportment and performed adequately, although not brilliantly, in her academic subjects.

In short, we can only agree with the conclusion that Dr. Lombardo has reached in his research on *Buck v. Bell*—there were no imbeciles, not a one, among the three generations of Bucks. I don't know that such correction of cruel but forgotten errors of history counts for much, but it is at least satisfying to learn that forced eugenic sterilization, a procedure of such dubious morality, earned its official justification (and won its most quoted line of rhetoric) on a patent falsehood.

Carrie Buck died [in 1983]. By a quirk of fate, and not by memory or design, she was buried just a few steps from her only daughter's grave. In the umpteenth and ultimate verse of a favorite old ballad, a rose and a brier—the sweet and the bitter—emerge from the tombs of Barbara Allen and her lover, twining about each other in the union of death. May Carrie and Vivian, victims in different ways and in the flower of youth, rest together in peace.

Buck v. Bell's Shameful Legacy

Center for Individual Freedom

*The following selection is taken from an article by the Center for
Individual Freedom, a nonprofit organization that works to protect individual rights guaranteed by the U.S. Constitution. The
essay places the case of* Buck v. Bell *in the context of the American eugenics movement of the early twentieth century. The writers contend that eugenics—the belief that the human race could
be improved through controlled breeding—was a pseudoscience
that was motivated in large part by racial and class prejudice.
Several states passed laws calling for the sterilization of people
deemed unfit, and these laws were given Supreme Court approval in the* Buck v. Bell *case. Between 1927 and 1979 more
than sixty-five thousand Americans were forcibly sterilized, according to the authors. America's system of sterilization also influenced the laws and actions of Nazi Germany. The writers note
that the eugenics movement has fallen into disfavor since the
1930s. On the seventy-fifth anniversary of the* Buck *decision,
Virginia governor Mark Warner formally apologized for his
state's role in that case. However, the authors also note that*
Buck v. Bell *remains part of U.S. law and indeed is still being
cited in some federal court cases.*

"It is better for all the world, if instead of waiting to execute
degenerate offspring for crime, or to let them starve for
their imbecility, society can prevent those who are mani-

Center for Individual Freedom, "The Sterilization of America: A Cautionary History,"
www.cfif.org, May 17, 2002. Copyright © 2002 by the Center for Individual Freedom.
Reproduced by permission.

festly unfit from continuing their kind. . . . Three generations of imbeciles are enough."

—*Supreme Court Justice Oliver Wendell Holmes, Jr.,*
in Buck v. Bell, 1927

Eugenics, a word all but removed from America's lexicon
after World War II, is the "science" of improving the human race through controlled breeding. . . . The word harkens
us back to a shameful time most would just as soon forget.

That task is made easier by today's politically-correct, sani-
tized text books in the nation's school systems; they will ensure the next generation of American utopians will never
know the pseudo-science which spawned Adolph Hitler's hor-
rific acts of ethnic cleansing was developed in American labo-
ratories, and upheld by the highest court in the land.

Origins of Eugenics

At the turn of the 20th century, the American industrial machine was moving full steam ahead, fueled by a burgeoning
working class and an endless influx of immigrants, mostly
from southern and eastern Europe. In an age of invention, scientists, doctors and economists were elevated to elite status, as
they churned out the latest economic and social theories of
the day. . . .

Progressive reformers sought a larger role for government
to address the growing inner-city issues of crime, poverty and
hunger that Industrialization left in its wake. For these social
"visionaries," who looked toward science to solve the problems
caused by a rapidly changing world, eugenics was a ready-
made tonic—prostitution, alcoholism, ignorance, birth defects, poverty, crime, could all be blamed on defective genes.

By 1883, Sir Francis Galton of Great Britain (Charles
Darwin's cousin) had coined the term eugenics—literally
meaning "well-born"—to apply to his groundbreaking theories on genetics and social engineering. Galton believed his

"moral philosophy" could improve the human species through encouraging society's best and brightest to have more children.

In the early 1900s, prominent American biologists Charles Davenport and Harry Laughlin, influenced by Galton, led other scientists and physicians in developing a radical brand of eugenics that argued for government to weed out degenerate members of the proletariat. Under the auspices of "social responsibility," involuntary sterilizations, genetic manipulation, race segregation and imprisonment were justified in order to save America from the high cost of treating defective individuals, who were responsible for the nation's social ills. In addition, immigration of "undesirables" could be curbed through selective genetic screening and strict immigration quotas.

Scientists and researchers with agricultural backgrounds flocked to the new field of eugenics. Inspired by animal and plant breeding practices, official records offices were opened by Davenport, Laughlin and others, to collect and catalog human pedigrees. Much like a public library, organizations such as the Eugenics Record Office (ERO) and the American Breeders Association (ABA), filled endless rows of card catalogs with detailed information on family lineages and physical and personality traits, such as moodiness or stubbornness. Also documented were mental and behavioral traits, such as alcoholism, epilepsy and depression. These offices also consulted young couples on suitable marriage partners and other matters of family planning.

The medical and scientific community worked overtime rolling out new studies to keep up with the need to support eugenicists' latest claims. Researchers, trained by eugenicists, combed asylums, prisons and orphanages across the country with questionnaires on family genealogies. Experts fanned out to cover the lecture and exhibit circuits with the slogan: "Some Americans are born to be a burden on the rest."

Steve Selden, author of *Inheriting Shame: The Story of Eugenics and Racism in America,* documents the effects eugenics had on popular culture. Hollywood movies covered the subject, as did religious services and well-known authors in books. State Fairs hosted "Fitter Families Contests," alongside the prized sow and biggest pumpkin contests. School curriculums from grade school to higher education included eugenics; top universities such as Harvard, Columbia, Cornell and Brown all offered courses on the "science."

Eugenical Sterilization Law

In 1907, Indiana became the first state to pass a law permitting involuntary sterilizations on eugenic grounds; at least 30 states would follow suit. Many of them simply adopted a model "eugenical sterilization law," crafted by the ERO's Harry Laughlin, which called for compulsory sterilizations of the "socially inadequate." By the mid-1920s, more than 3,000 people had been sterilized against their wills. These included the homeless, orphans, epileptics, the blind and deaf. Also sterilized were those who scored poorly on IQ tests, who were diagnosed as being "feebleminded."

During that time, Congress also got into the act. Hearings were held by the Committee on Immigration and Naturalization in the House of Representatives to investigate claims that eastern European countries were intentionally "exporting" degenerates to America. Effective lobbying by Harry Laughlin, an "expert agent" for the committee, led to the passage of anti-immigration laws with strict country quotas that favored northern and western European nations.

"Three Generations of Imbeciles"

In 1924, a teenager in Charlottesville, Virginia, Carrie Buck, was chosen as the first person to be sterilized under the state's newly adopted eugenics law. Ms. Buck, whose mother resided in an asylum for the epileptic and feebleminded, was accused of having a child out of wedlock. She was diagnosed as promiscuous and the probable parent of "socially inadequate offspring."

A lawsuit challenging the sterilization was filed on Ms. Buck's behalf. Harry Laughlin, having never met Ms. Buck, wrote a deposition condemning her and her 7-month-old child, Vivian. Scientists from the ERO attended the trial to testify to Vivian's "backwardness." In the end, the judge ruled in the state's favor.

On appeal, the U.S. Supreme Court in the landmark case *Buck v. Bell* (1927), ruled 8-1 to uphold the sterilization of Ms. Buck on the grounds she was a "deficient" mother. [Associate] Justice Oliver Wendell Holmes Jr., an adherent of eugenics, declared "Three generations of imbeciles are enough."

According to University of Virginia historian Paul Lombardo, evidence was later revealed that supports the claim that Carrie Buck's child was not the result of promiscuity; Ms. Buck had been raped by the nephew of her foster parents. School records also indicate her daughter Vivian was a solid student and had made the honor roll at age 7. A year later, Vivian died of an intestinal illness.

The Aftermath

By the late 1930s, the study of eugenics began to lose its luster in America. Increasingly, independent scientists began disproving eugenicists' claims. Earlier data was revealed to be skewed and biased towards Americans of western European descent, particularly those inhabiting New England states. By 1939, financial support from individuals and foundations, such as cereal maker J.H. Kellogg and Mrs. E.H. Harriman, the wife of a railway magnate, had dried up and the Eugenics Records Office was forced to close its doors. However, involuntary sterilizations continued in this country through the late 1970s.

May 2, 2002, marked the 75th anniversary of the shameful *Buck v. Bell* decision, which has never been overruled and was cited in a federal appeals case as recently as [2001].[1] The Court's action in *Buck* led to the forced sterilization of more than 65,000 Americans by 1979. To mark the anniversary of the *Buck* decision, Virginia Governor Mark Warner formally apologized for his state's role saying: "The eugenics movement was a shameful effort in which state government never should have been involved."

As for the legacy of Harry Laughlin, his model law was adopted by Nazi Germany in 1934 and led to the sterilization of 350,000 German "feebleminded" people. In 1936, Laughlin was honored with a degree from the University of Heidelberg for his efforts in eugenics. By 1940, Germany adopted a policy of euthanasia for German children and adults with birth defects and mental disorders. In 1941, "special actions" were ordered to exterminate Jews, gypsies, and other "undesirable elements."

What Tomorrow May Bring

The eugenics issue has begun to rear its ugly head once again on the politically explosive issues of immigration quotas, embryo research and human cloning. Bioethicists and religious opponents lob accusations at genetic scientists, saying they are "playing God" or seeking to create "designer babies." Germany, which is still haunted by its history of Nazi eugenics, has banned its scientists from most embryonic research and creating cloned embryos. . . .

If we are not careful, the current push in this country for biometrics—the use of genetic markers, facial recognition, hand-scanning, fingerprint scanning and eye scanning for identification purposes—may provide a database for future generations who, ignorant of the past, may be condemned to repeat it.

1. In *Vaughn v. Ruoff* (2001), the judges cited *Buck* and asserted that "involuntary sterilization is not always unconstitutional if it is a narrowly tailored means to achieve a compelling government interest."

CHAPTER 2

Legalizing Contraception

Case Overview

Griswold v. Connecticut (1965)

In *Griswold v. Connecticut*, the United States Supreme Court struck down state laws forbidding the use of contraceptives by married couples. The ruling has been both praised and attacked for articulating a constitutional "right of privacy" that protects the personal decision whether to use birth control.

Although contraceptives have been used throughout human history, a significant turning point in their development was the invention of the oral contraceptive. The "Pill" was approved for use in the United States in 1960; by 1963 2.3 million American women were using this new form of birth control. However, several states still had laws on the books that restricted or banned the sale and/or use of all contraceptives. One of the most stringent was an 1879 Connecticut law that made both the use of contraceptives and the act of helping people obtain or use contraceptives punishable crimes. In 1961 Estelle T. Griswold, executive director of Planned Parenthood League of Connecticut, and C. Lee Buxton, the chair of Yale University School of Medicine's Obstetrics Department, opened a clinic in New Haven in which birth control information and devices were provided to married couples. In setting up their practice, they openly defied Connecticut's laws—laws they intended to challenge in court as violations of their constitutional rights of free speech and due process of law.

Griswold and Buxton were arrested in November 1961 and put on trial in January 1962. They were convicted of violating Connecticut's anticontraceptive laws; their convictions were upheld on appeal. Associate Justice John Comley of the Connecticut Supreme Court of Errors in May 1964 declared: "We adhere to the principle that courts may not interfere with the exercise by a state of the policy power to conserve the public safety and welfare, including health and morals."

The case was appealed and argued before the U.S. Supreme Court in 1964. The Court issued its 7-2 decision on June 7, 1965. A majority reversed Griswold's and Buxton's convictions and invalidated the 1879 law as a violation of a married couple's right to privacy. Its ruling drew controversy both then and since in part because the phrase "right to privacy" does not appear in the Constitution. However, a majority of justices held that several constitutional amendments and phrases created "zones of privacy" which, taken together, added up to a constitutional right to privacy.

The principles behind *Griswold* influenced later important Supreme Court reproductive rights cases. In *Eisenstadt v. Baird* (1972), the Supreme Court ruled that single people, in addition to married couples, had a constitutional right to purchase and use birth control. In *Roe v. Wade* (1973), the right to privacy first established in *Griswold* was extended to encompass a woman's right to make the decision to have an abortion.

> "We deal with a right of privacy older
> than the Bill of Rights."

The Court's Decision: Laws Banning Birth Control Are Unconstitutional

William O. Douglas

William O. Douglas served on the Supreme Court from 1939 to 1975. Appointed by Franklin D. Roosevelt, Douglas became known as one of the most liberal voices on the Court and a strong supporter of civil liberties. He wrote and delivered the majority opinion in the case of Griswold v. Connecticut *(1965), excerpted here. The Court, by a 7-2 majority, ruled that an 1879 Connecticut state law banning both the use and the provision of contraceptive drugs or devices was unconstitutional because it interfered with marriage and violated the people's "right of privacy." Douglas argues that while neither birth control nor privacy are explicitly mentioned in the Constitution or Bill of Rights, provisions in both documents create "zones of privacy" that should be recognized and protected.*

Appellant Griswold is Executive Director of the Planned Parenthood League of Connecticut. Appellant Buxton is a licensed physician and a professor at the Yale Medical School who served as Medical Director for the League at its Center in New Haven—a center open and operating from November 1 to November 10, 1961, when appellants were arrested.

They gave information, instruction, and medical advice to *married persons* as to the means of preventing conception. They examined the wife and prescribed the best contraceptive device or material for her use. Fees were usually charged, although some couples were serviced free. . . .

William O. Douglas, majority opinion, *Griswold v. Connecticut,* June 7, 1965.

The statutes whose constitutionality is involved in this appeal are §§ 53–32 and 54–196 of the General Statutes of Connecticut (1958 rev.). The Former provides:

> "Any person who uses any drug, medicinal article or instrument for the purpose of preventing conception shall be fined not less than fifty dollars or imprisoned not less than sixty days nor more than one year or be both fined and imprisoned."

Section 54–196 provides:

> "Any person who assists, abets, counsels, causes, hires or commands another to commit any offense may be prosecuted and punished as if he were the principal offender."

The appellants were found guilty as accessories and fined $100 each, against the claim that the accessory statute as so applied violated the Fourteenth Amendment. . . .

We are met with a wide range of questions that implicate the Due Process Clause of the Fourteenth Amendment. . . . We do not sit as a super-legislature to determine the wisdom, need, and propriety of laws that touch economic problems, business affairs, or social conditions. This law, however, operates directly on an intimate relation of husband and wife and their physician's role in one aspect of that relation.

Recognized Rights

The association of people is not mentioned in the Constitution nor in the Bill of Rights. The right to educate a child in a school of the parents' choice—whether public or private or parochial—is also not mentioned. Nor is the right to study any particular subject or any foreign language. Yet the First Amendment has been construed to include certain of those rights.

By *Pierce v. Society of Sisters,* the right to educate one's children as one chooses is made applicable to the States by the force of the First and Fourteenth Amendments. By *Meyer v. Nebraska,* the same dignity is given the right to study the German language in a private school. In other words, the State may not, consistently with the spirit of the First Amendment, contract the spectrum of available knowledge. The right of freedom of speech and press includes not only the right to utter or to print, but the right to distribute, the right to receive, the right to read, and freedom of inquiry, freedom of thought, and freedom to teach. . . . Without those peripheral rights the specific rights would be less secure. And so we reaffirm the principle of the *Pierce* and the *Meyer* cases.

In *NAACP v. Alabama,* we protected the "freedom to associate and privacy in one's associations," noting that freedom of association was a peripheral First Amendment right. Disclosure of membership lists of a constitutionally valid association, we held, was invalid "as entailing the likelihood of a substantial restraint upon the exercise by petitioner's members of their right to freedom of association." In other words, the First Amendment has a penumbra where privacy is protected from governmental intrusion. In like context, we have protected forms of "association" that are not political in the customary sense but pertain to the social, legal, and economic benefit of the members. . . .

The right of "association," like the right of belief (*Board of Education v. Barnette*), is more than the right to attend a meeting; it includes the right to express one's attitudes or philosophies by membership in a group or by affiliation with it or by other lawful means. Association in that context is a form of expression of opinion; and while it is not expressly included in the First Amendment its existence is necessary in making the express guarantees fully meaningful.

Penumbras

The foregoing cases suggest that specific guarantees in the Bill of Rights have penumbras, formed by emanations from those guarantees that help give them life and substance. . . . Various guarantees create zones of privacy. The right of association contained in the penumbra of the First Amendment is one, as we have seen. The Third Amendment in its prohibition against the quartering of soldiers "in any house" in time of peace without the consent of the owner is another facet of that privacy. The Fourth Amendment explicitly affirms the "right of the people to be secure in their persons, houses, papers, and effects, against unreasonable searches and seizures." The Fifth Amendment in its Self-Incrimination Clause enables the citizen to create a zone of privacy which government may not force him to surrender to his detriment. The Ninth Amendment provides: "The enumeration in the Constitution, of certain rights, shall not be construed to deny or disparage others retained by the people." . . .

The present case, then, concerns a relationship lying within the zone of privacy created by several fundamental constitutional guarantees. And it concerns a law which, in forbidding the *use* of contraceptives rather than regulating their manufacture or sale, seeks to achieve its goals by means having a maximum destructive impact upon that relationship. Such a law cannot stand in light of the familiar principle, so often applied by this Court, that a "governmental purpose to control or prevent activities constitutionally subject to state regulation may not be achieved by means which sweep unnecessarily broadly and thereby invade the area of protected freedoms" (*NAACP v. Alabama*). Would we allow the police to search the sacred precincts of marital bedrooms for telltale signs of the use of contraceptives? The very idea is repulsive to the notions of privacy surrounding the marriage relationship.

We deal with a right of privacy older than the Bill of Rights—older than our political parties, older than our school system. Marriage is a coming together for better or worse, hopefully enduring, and intimate to the degree of being sacred. It is an association that promotes a way of life, not causes; a harmony in living, not political faiths; a bilateral loyalty, not commercial or social projects. Yet it is an association for as noble a purpose as any involved in our prior decisions.

> "We are not asked in this case to say whether we think this law is unwise. . . . We are asked to hold that it violates the United States Constitution. And that I cannot do."

Dissenting Opinion: There Is No Constitutional Right to Birth Control

Potter Stewart

Potter Stewart was one of two dissenting justices in Griswold v. Connecticut, *the 1965 case in which the U.S. Supreme Court ruled that state laws banning contraceptive use were unconstitutional. In the following viewpoint, excerpted from his dissenting opinion, Stewart argues that while the Connecticut state law banning contraceptives is "uncommonly silly," there is nothing in the Constitution, including the Bill of Rights, that creates a general right of privacy or authorizes the Supreme Court to overturn the law. The constitutional method of repealing birth control laws, Stewart concludes, is through the action of elected public legislators. Stewart served as an associate justice of the Supreme Court from 1958 to 1981.*

Since 1879 Connecticut has had on its books a law which forbids the use of contraceptives by anyone. I think this is an uncommonly silly law. As a practical matter, the law is obviously unenforceable, except in the oblique context of the present case. As a philosophical matter, I believe the use of contraceptives in the relationship of marriage should be left to personal and private choice, based upon each individual's

Potter Stewart, dissenting opinion, *Griswold v. Connecticut,* June 7, 1965.

moral, ethical, and religious beliefs. As a matter of social policy, I think professional counsel about methods of birth control should be available to all, so that each individual's choice can be meaningfully made. But we are not asked in this case to say whether we think this law is unwise, or even asinine. We are asked to hold that it violates the United States Constitution. And that I cannot do.

Nothing in the Constitution

In the course of its opinion the Court refers to no less than six Amendments to the Constitution: the First, the Third, the Fourth, the Fifth, the Ninth, and the Fourteenth. But the Court does not say which of these Amendments, if any, it thinks is infringed by this Connecticut law. We *are* told that the Due Process Clause of the Fourteenth Amendment is not, as such, the "guide" in this case. With that much I agree. There is no claim that this law, duly enacted by the Connecticut Legislature, is unconstitutionally vague. There is no claim that the appellants were denied any of the elements of procedural due process at their trial, so as to make their convictions constitutionally invalid. And, as the Court says, the day has long passed since the Due Process Clause was regarded as a proper instrument for determining "the wisdom, need, and propriety" of state laws. . . .

As to the First, Third, Fourth, and Fifth Amendments, I can find nothing in any of them to invalidate this Connecticut law, even assuming that all those Amendments are fully applicable against the States. It has not even been argued that this is a law [in the words of the First Amendment] "respecting an establishment of religion, or prohibiting the free exercise thereof." And surely, unless the solemn process of constitutional adjudication is to descend to the level of a play on words, there is not involved here any abridgment of [again, as stated by the First Amendment] "the freedom of speech, or of the press; or the right of the people peaceably to assemble, and to petition the Government for a redress of grievances." No soldier has been quartered in any house. There has been no search, and no seizure. Nobody has been compelled to be a witness against himself [as provided by the Third, Fourth, and Fifth Amendments, respectively].

The Court also quotes the Ninth Amendment, and my Brother [Justice Arthur] Goldberg's concurring opinion relies heavily upon it. But to say that the Ninth Amendment has anything to do with this case is to turn somersaults with history. The Ninth Amendment . . . was framed by James Madison and adopted by the States simply to make clear that the adoption of the Bill of Rights did not alter the plan that the *Federal* Government was to be a government of express and limited powers, and that all rights and powers not delegated to it were retained by the people and the individual States. Until today no member of this Court has ever suggested that the Ninth Amendment meant anything else, and the idea that a federal court could ever use the Ninth Amendment to annul a law passed by the elected representatives of the people of the State of Connecticut would have caused James Madison no little wonder.

What provision of the Constitution, then, does make this state law invalid? The Court says it is the right of privacy "created by several fundamental constitutional guarantees." With all deference, I can find no such general right of privacy in the Bill of Rights, in any other part of the Constitution, or in any case ever before decided by this Court.

People Are Free to Change the Law

At the oral argument in this case we were told that the Connecticut law does not "conform to current community standards." But it is not the function of this Court to decide cases on the basis of community standards. We are here to decide cases "agreeably to the Constitution and laws of the United States." It is the essence of judicial duty to subordinate our own personal views, our own ideas of what legislation is wise and what is not. If, as I should surely hope, the law before us does not reflect the standards of the people of Connecticut, the people of Connecticut can freely exercise their true Ninth and Tenth Amendment rights to persuade their elected representatives to repeal it. That is the constitutional way to take this law off the books.

"The Supreme Court was finally able to decide an issue which had smoldered for years."

The *Griswold* Decision Was an Overdue Ruling on Archaic Contraception Laws

Commonweal

Commonweal *is a weekly public affairs journal that is aimed at a Roman Catholic readership but is not an official church publication. The following selection is a* Commonweal *editorial published shortly after the 1965* Griswold v. Connecticut *decision. The authors argue that the Supreme Court's decision overturning Connecticut's laws against contraceptives was "long overdue." Such laws, they contend, are anachronistic, impossible to enforce, and do not reflect the public consensus. They further contend that Roman Catholic teachings on the immorality of birth control should not dictate the content of government laws.*

The action of the Supreme Court on June 7 [1965], declaring the Connecticut birth control law unconstitutional, was long overdue. Put on the books by Protestants in [1879], the law in recent years was maintained there primarily by Catholics. On the face of it, the law was, as one justice noted, just plain silly. It not only forbade the sale and distribution of contraceptives, it also made their use by married couples a criminal act. Naturally, this latter provision of the law was never enforced in recent decades. How could it be? But beyond that, it was an open secret that one could buy contra-

Commonweal, "The Connecticut Decision," vol. LXXXII, June 25, 1965, pp. 427–28. Copyright © 1965 by Commonweal Publishing Co., Inc. Reproduced by permission of the Commonweal Foundation.

ceptives with ease in any neighborhood drug store. The only people who felt the sting of the law were some members of the Planned Parenthood League who opened a birth control clinic in New Haven. In overturning their conviction by the courts of Connecticut, the Supreme Court was finally able to decide an issue which had smouldered for years.

From a legal point of view, the decision was a muddy one. As the two dissenters, Justice[s] [Potter] Stewart and [Hugo] Black, were quick to point out, the majority of the Court had some difficulty locating an amendment which would provide a clear constitutional basis for the decision. Justice [William O.] Douglas' argument that "We deal with a right to privacy older than the Bill of Rights" is morally persuasive, but hardly designed to placate those who fear the Court has once again set itself up as a supreme legislative, rather than judicial body. For the moment, we leave that debate to others.

Public Policy Implications

Of more immediate concern is the meaning of the decision for public policy. Though Connecticut was the only state which forbade the use of contraceptives, there still remain five others which totally prohibit their sale and advertisement, and eight more which forbid only their advertisement. With the exception, perhaps, of open advertising and sales to minors it is unlikely that any of these laws would remain on the books but for the opposition of Catholics. In practice, most of these laws are dead letters, unenforced and unheeded. Thus a *de facto* compromise is in effect. Some Catholics are able to have the solace of seeing their natural law convictions recognized by the civil law, while non-Catholics are unimpeded in doing what they see fit.

And that of course is a silly situation also. It makes a mockery of the idea of civil law, which should rest on public consensus or constitutional rights. To find a Catholic moral theologian who will any longer defend such laws would likely be a vain search. To find a non-Catholic who happily accepts the existence of such laws would be no less arduous a hunt. Yet the hue and cry continues to persist whenever state legislatures try to remove these anachronistic statutes. There is always some obscure Catholic "spokesman," often fronting for the local chancery, who fights to keep them on the books.

Why is this? The reason, we fear, has little to do with moral convictions and a careful weighing of the rights of majority and minority groups. Instead, it too often stems from a fear of the impact a change in the laws would have on discipline within the Church. If Church authorities agree to a change in the law, then—the argument goes—this will appear tantamount to a change in the Church's moral convictions on the issue. Once again that classic Catholic figure is evoked: the simple, unlettered peasant who is inherently incapable of grasping the theologian's distinction between moral and civil law. What ain't agin the law is OK—that's the way he is supposed to reason.

An Unnecessary Court Struggle

That man died long ago. And even if he has some descendants, the Church's pastoral problem of reaching their conscience should not be solved by sustaining laws which offend the moral sensibilities of non-Catholics. Who is fooled anyway? To discover there even exist anti-contraceptive laws in many states requires education and sophistication, but even the most ignorant know you can buy contraceptives anywhere.

If there was anything clearly unfortunate about the Supreme Court decision, it was the fact that a constitutional decision was required in the first place. With no violation whatever even of the most hoary Catholic jurisprudential principles, the Connecticut hierarchy could have ceased long ago opposing the almost yearly attempts to have the law changed in the Connecticut legislature. (The same can be said of similar obstructionist tactics in Massachusetts.) The entire round of court struggles was unnecessary, a dubious tribute to the power of a determined minority to impose their moral values on others. Will it happen again somewhere? Probably, for the Catholic community has learned its lessons slowly and in the hard way. The Supreme Court is an expensive tutor.

> "Those who regard the invasion of the individual's privacy . . . as one of the great threats of our time may come to regard the Griswold case as the Magna Charta of the 20th century."

Griswold Expanded Individual Rights

James D. Carroll

At the time this essay was first published, in 1965, James D. Carroll was a resident at the Maxwell School in Syracuse University. He later chaired the Department of Public Administration at Syracuse and served as a senior staff member at the Brookings Institution. He is currently a professor of public policy and administration at Florida International University. In the following viewpoint he makes several predictions about the impact of Griswold v. Connecticut, *in which the Supreme Court struck down a state law against using or disseminating contraceptives as a violation of marital privacy. Carroll notes that the language of the ruling could also be used to strike down compulsory birth control laws that were at the time being openly discussed as a possible solution to human population growth. He also predicts that the Court's recognition of a general right to privacy and its use of the Ninth Amendment may influence future cases in which the Court weighs the extent of privacy rights.*

In *Griswold v. Connecticut,* the birth-control case handed down on June 7 [1965], the Supreme Court confounded most of the informed members of its public by giving everyone something and no one everything. . . .

James D. Carroll, "The Forgotten Amendment . . ." *The Nation,* vol. 201, September 6, 2003, pp. 121–22. Copyright © 2003 by The Nation Magazine/The Nation Company, Inc. Reproduced by permission.

The Court's Decision

The Court's decision was clear and simple: seven members agreed that the Connecticut statute prohibiting the dissemination and use of birth-control information and devices is unconstitutional. The grounds on which the decision was reached were not so simple: the statute violates a right to marital privacy that is fundamental to our civilization and our way of life. To explain their reasoning, the seven members of the Court who agreed with the decision produced four opinions. The dissenting Justices [Hugo] Black and [Potter] Stewart produced two. June 7 was a good day for those who like to read Supreme Court opinions.

It is evident that the appellants, Estelle T. Griswold and Dr. Charles Lee Buxton, had got what they wanted. The Planned Parenthood League's birth-control clinic in New Haven can now legally disseminate birth-control information and devices. The citizens of Connecticut can now practice birth control in peace. But the appellants paid for this victory, if not out of their own intellectual pockets, then out of the intellectual pockets of those who believe that some form of compulsory birth control will be necessary in the future. The price they paid was the Court's recognition of marital privacy as a right that transcends the social interests of the state. Three of the Court's liberals, Chief Justice [Earl] Warren, Justice [Arthur] Goldberg and Justice [William] Brennan, went far out of their way to state flatly that a law requiring compulsory birth control would be just as unconstitutional as the Connecticut law outlawing voluntary birth control, since both laws would violate the right of marital privacy. This observation was a dictum, of course, but it was no idle or academic dictum, nor was it a sop tossed to the beggars who wanted the Connecticut law upheld.

These Justices expressed an acute awareness that many people in the United States and elsewhere are convinced that some form of compulsory birth control is inevitable. For example, Kenneth Boulding, who is widely and I think rightly respected as a thinker of prescience and insight, recently outlined the world's population problem and explained his response to it: "I think in all seriousness," Boulding wrote in *The Meaning of the Twentieth Century,* "that a system of marketable licenses to have children is the only one which will combine the minimum of social control necessary to the solution to this problem with a maximum of individual liberty and ethical choice." Boulding's plan may seem absurd at the moment, but who fifty years ago could foresee that in the 1960s the Catholic Church would re-examine its stand on artificial birth control?

A Right to Privacy

The grounds of the Court's decision should satisfy many citizens who wanted the Court to leave the Connecticut statute alone. Even those who think the Court should quit playing the role of interpreter of the American conscience should be pleased with the majority's affirmation of a right to marital privacy and with the clear suggestion that the majority will recognize other forms of a general right to privacy in the future.

Prior to the birth-control decision, a right to privacy had to be tagged on to one of the specific rights affirmed in the First, Third, Fourth, Fifth or Sixth Amendments. If the action of a state were involved, the right had to be arrived at through interpretation of the due process clause of the Fourteenth Amendment. A central issue in the case was this: Is there a constitutional right to privacy that applies to both state and federal action involving relationships not enumerated in the Constitution?

The majority of the Court held yes. The majority flatly stated that a constitutionally protected "zone of privacy" against state and federal action exists, a zone not limited to the exact relationships specified in specific constitutional provisions. In cases of state action, this zone of privacy is guaranteed both by the due process clause of the Fourteenth Amendment and by the Ninth Amendment. In cases of federal action it is guaranteed by the entire Bill of Rights.

The boundaries of the zone of privacy will have to be defined in future cases. Those who regard the invasion of the individual's privacy through the collectivization of man as one of the great threats of our time may come to regard the Griswold case as the Magna Charta of the 20th century. In more modest terms, they may derive immediate solace from Justice [William O.] Douglas' concluding words of the Court's opinion:

> We deal with a right of privacy older than the Bill of Rights—older than our political parties, older than our school system. Marriage is a coming together for better or for worse, hopefully enduring, and intimate to the degree of being sacred. The association promotes a way of life, not causes; a harmony in living, not political faiths; a bilateral loyalty, not commercial or social projects.

The Ninth Amendment

To the student of constitutional history, perhaps the most interesting aspect of the birth-control case is the Court's recognition of the Ninth Amendment as a mechanism for the expression of "the collective conscience of our people" against both federal and state action. The Ninth Amendment reads: "The enumeration in the Constitution, of certain rights, shall not be construed to deny or disparage others retained by the people." The recognition at this time of the Ninth Amendment as a substantive limitation on state and federal action is truly an astounding development. As Bennett B. Patterson pointed out ten years ago in the *Forgotten Ninth Amendment,* the Supreme Court throughout its entire history has almost completely ignored the Ninth Amendment.

As far as I can determine from a recent check of Supreme Court cases, the Court never in its entire history has decided a single case on the basis of the Ninth Amendment. It has discussed the Ninth Amendment in half a dozen cases. In one of these, *United Public Workers v. Mitchell,* it used the Ninth Amendment to support a decision arrived at on other grounds. Throughout most of its history, the Court has apparently accepted the traditional understanding of the amendment expressed by Justice Stewart in his dissenting opinion in the birth-control case. Justice Stewart argued that the Ninth Amendment was adopted merely to make clear that the adoption of the Bill of Rights did not alter the plan that the federal government is a government of express and limited powers. "Until today, no member of this Court has ever suggested that the Ninth Amendment meant anything else. . . ."

Justice Goldberg expressed the new meaning of the Ninth Amendment in his concurring opinion. He argued that the language and history of the Ninth Amendment reveal that the framers of the Constitution believed that other fundamental rights which are protected against government infringement exist alongside the rights specifically mentioned in the first eight amendments to the Constitution. The Ninth Amendment recognizes that these fundamental personal rights, such as the right to marital privacy, are protected from abridgment by government though not specifically mentioned in the Constitution. The courts must look to the "collective conscience of our people" to determine whether a principle is so rooted there as to be ranked as fundamental.

The recognition by the Court of the Ninth Amendment is of fundamental importance as an affirmation of the Court's intention to protect the sovereignty and dignity of the individual. In a way, this recognition constitutes the declaration of a new Bill of Rights for the 20th century for as Patterson said in his prophetic book:

There is no clause in the Constitution, except the Ninth Amendment, which makes a declaration of the sovereignty and dignity of the individual.

Since individual freedom is the basis of democracy, and is the virtue which marks the excellence of our form of government over all other forms of government ... the Ninth Amendment immediately takes its place as the most important declaration in our Constitution, because such a declaration is nowhere else therein to be found.

Who won the birth-control case? All of the parties to the case, both immediate and remote, lost something, but I personally think that in the Court's recognition of a constitutional right of privacy and in the Court's recognition of the Ninth Amendment, everyone gained a lot.

The Supreme Court Had No Valid Justification for Legalizing Contraception

Mark R. Levin

Mark R. Levin is a lawyer, radio talk show host, and author of
Men in Black: How the Supreme Court Is Destroying America,
*from which the following viewpoint is excerpted. He argues that
the Supreme Court in* Griswold v. Connecticut *created a general right to privacy that does not exist in the text of the Constitution. In that case and in others involving birth control and
abortion, the Supreme Court acted improperly by interjecting its
views into the debate over reproductive rights. Contraception,
abortion, and other controversial social issues should be decided
by the legislative branch of government, not by unelected judges,
Levin concludes.*

Today, legalized abortion is the law of the land because the
Supreme Court decided in 1973 that its recently created
constitutional right to privacy also included a new constitutional right to abortion. If you look in the Constitution, however, you will find no general "right to privacy" any more than
you will find a right to abortion—and for good reason: It's
not there. The framers assumed no general right to privacy
because, to state the obvious, criminal and evil acts can be

committed in privacy. Criminal codes are full of such examples—from murder to incest to rape and other crimes.

The *Poe* Precedent

The modern argument for a right to privacy began in 1961 in Justice John Marshall Harlan's dissent in *Poe v. Ullman.* The case was brought by Planned Parenthood on behalf of a carefully selected group of people: a married couple, a single woman, and a Planned Parenthood obstetrician, C. Lee Buxton. Planned Parenthood's suit was directed against a Connecticut law that prohibited the sale and use of contraceptives. The Supreme Court dismissed the case because the law had not been enforced against the people in Planned Parenthood's case. It is a basic judicial principle that there has to be an actual legal dispute to be adjudicated. But Justice Harlan issued a dissent, writing, "I believe that a statute making it a criminal offense for married couples to use contraceptives is an intolerable and unjustifiable invasion of privacy in the conduct of the most intimate concerns of an individual's personal life."

Harlan provided an extensive rationale for his position, which became the theoretical cornerstone for the right to privacy. Where did Harlan derive his notions about privacy rights? Melvin L. Wulf, a lawyer for the American Civil Liberties Union, claims credit for first raising the idea with Harlan in the ACLU's friend-of-the court brief in *Poe v. Ullman.* Wulf later explained his strategy for getting the Court to adopt the privacy rights approach:

> Judges dislike breaking entirely new ground. If they are considering adopting a novel principle, they prefer to rest their decision on earlier law if they can, and to show that the present case involves merely an incremental change, not a wholesale break with the past. Constitutional litigators are forever trying to persuade courts that the result they are seeking would be just a short step from some other case whose decision rests soundly on ancient precedent.

Since the issue of sexual privacy had not been raised in any earlier case, we employed the familiar technique of argument by analogy: If there is no exact counterpart to the particular case before the Court, there are others that resemble it in a general sort of way, and the principles applied in the similar cases should also be applied—*perhaps even extended a little bit*—to the new case. [Emphasis added (by Levin).]

Making Privacy Constitutional

In other words, Wulf understood that the Court would be open to rewriting the Constitution by pretending to uphold it. Although Harlan's was a minority opinion, and had no immediate legal effect, its impact would soon become clear. After *Poe* was decided, Planned Parenthood officials found a way to get arrested so they could mount another challenge to Connecticut law. In 1965, Justice William O. Douglas adopted Harlan's reasoning in the majority opinion in the case of *Griswold v. Connecticut,* and the right to privacy became constitutional law. Douglas, who was appointed by President Franklin Roosevelt in 1939, is most famous for being the longest-serving justice and, to conservatives, for writing one of the most parodied phrases in Supreme Court history. In order to strike down the Connecticut law prohibiting the sale of contraceptives, Douglas wrote that "specific guarantees in the Bill of Rights have penumbras, formed by emanations from those guarantees that help give them life and substance."

Don't be embarrassed if you don't know what emanations from penumbras are. Young lawyers across America had to pull out their dictionaries when reading *Griswold* for the first time. A penumbra is an astronomical term describing the partial shadow in an eclipse or the edge of a sunspot—and it is another way to describe something unclear or uncertain. "Emanation" is a scientific term for gas made from radioactive decay—it also means "an emission."

Manipulation of Facts

Douglas's decision not only found a right to privacy in a penumbra of an emanation, it manipulated the facts of the case: Estelle Griswold, the executive director of the Planned Parenthood League of Connecticut, and Dr. C. Lee Buxton, the group's medical director, gave information and prescribed birth control to a married couple. Griswold and Buxton, not the married couple, were later convicted and fined $100 each. The relationship at issue, then, was doctor-patient, not husband-wife. Yet Douglas framed his opinion around a presumed right to *marital* privacy. He expounded at length about the sanctity of marriage but used vague phrasing to describe the rights at issue, never explicitly stating that married couples have a right to use contraceptives. He even raised the ugly specter of sex police, though no police had intruded into anyone's bedroom. "Would we allow the police to search the sacred precincts of marital bedrooms for telltale signs of the use of contraceptives?" This little phrase has been used as holy writ by judicial activists ever since to further expand the right to privacy in a variety of areas, including abortion and sodomy. . . .

Justice Hugo Black, in his dissent, was not impressed. He attacked the way Douglas had turned constitutional law into semantics by replacing the language of actual rights with the phrase "right to privacy." He wrote, "The Court talks about a constitutional 'right of privacy' as though there is some constitutional provision or provisions forbidding any law ever to be passed which might abridge the 'privacy' of individuals. But there is not. There are, of course, guarantees in certain specific constitutional provisions which are designed in part to protect privacy at certain times and places with respect to certain activities."

Black, normally an ally of Douglas, feared that using such a phrase as "right to privacy" could be a double-edged sword. "One of the most effective ways of diluting or expanding a constitutionally guaranteed right is to substitute for the crucial word or words of a constitutional guarantee another word or words, more or less flexible and more or less restricted in meaning. . . . 'Privacy' is a broad, abstract and ambiguous concept which can easily be shrunken in meaning but which can also, on the other hand, easily be interpreted as a constitutional ban against many things other than searches and seizures." Black concluded by saying, "I like my privacy as well as the next one, but I am nevertheless compelled to admit that government has a right to invade it unless prohibited by some specific constitutional provision."

Extending Contraceptive Rights to Unmarried Couples

Seven years after the issue of married couples and contraceptives was decided in *Griswold,* the Court considered contraceptives and unmarried couples in 1972 in *Eisenstadt v. Baird.* Although he quoted *Griswold* frequently in the majority opinion, Justice William Brennan nonetheless found that Massachusetts law could be overturned on Fourteenth Amendment equal protection grounds without having to rely on the marital privacy rights created by *Griswold.* While Connecticut's law in *Griswold* prohibited the use of contraceptives, Massachusetts had laws restricting their distribution. Married people could obtain contraceptives only from doctors or pharmacists by prescription, while single people could obtain them only to prevent the spread of disease. Massachusetts law was challenged when William Baird gave a speech at Boston University about birth control and overpopulation. He exhibited contraceptives and gave "Emko vaginal foam" to a young woman in the audience, both of which actions were illegal, and Baird was convicted. His conviction for showing contraceptives was overturned by the Massachusetts Supreme Judicial Court on First Amendment grounds, so distribution was the sole issue before the U.S. Supreme Court.

Brennan found that the statute was a prohibition on contraception per se and ruled that "whatever the rights of the individual to access contraceptives may be, the rights must be the same for the unmarried and the married alike." Yet again, a major Supreme Court decision rested on a naked assertion of opinion instead of legal reasoning. Nowhere does the Constitution require that married couples and single people be treated the same where contraception is involved.

Brennan then argued for expanding the right to privacy: "If under *Griswold* the distribution of contraceptives to married persons cannot be prohibited, a ban on distribution to unmarried persons would be equally impermissible. It is true that in *Griswold* the right of privacy in question inhered in the marital relationship. Yet the marital couple is not an independent entity with a mind and heart of its own, but an association of two individuals each with a separate intellectual and emotional makeup."

In other words, Douglas's rhetoric about the sanctity of marriage was essentially irrelevant. The right to privacy belonged to individuals, not the couple.

Brennan continued, "If the right of privacy means anything, it is the right of the individual, married or single, to be free from unwarranted governmental intrusion into matters so fundamentally affecting a person as the decision whether to bear or beget a child."

Usurping the Legislature's Authority

So the right to privacy means everything and nothing. It has no constitutional basis and no tangible form. But what is clear is that the Supreme Court, by usurping the legislature's authority to set social policy, has seized from the people the power to make such determinations. A mere five justices are now able to substitute their personal judgments for those of Congress and every state government in the name of privacy rights. This quiet revolution against representative government has gone largely unnoticed. The exception is the occasional Court decision on "hot button" issues in which the attention is mostly on the Court's ruling, not on its abuse of power.

Also notice how Brennan inserted the phrase to "bear or beget a child" in the opinion. The case was about contraceptives, which affect only the begetting of children. Yet Brennan explicitly added the concept of bearing a child as well. He was subtly laying the foundation to extend the right of privacy to encompass the right to abortion. This occurred at a time when *Roe v. Wade*—a case involving abortion—had twice been argued before the Court but had not yet been decided. Notice how the judicial activists work—inserting a word in a majority opinion here and there, inserting a phrase in a dissenting opinion, all the while biding their time until five justices can be convinced to join the cause.

"Griswold v. Connecticut . . . *profoundly deepened the constitutional right of individuals to be free from government intrusion in their own private lives.*"

Griswold Helped Secure Americans' Reproductive Rights

Elizabeth Borg

June 7, 2005, marked the fortieth anniversary of the Griswold v. Connecticut *decision that overturned a Connecticut state law banning contraception. In the following selection, originally written to commemorate this milestone, Elizabeth Borg praises the Supreme Court's actions in* Griswold. *She argues that the decision affirmed the right to use birth control and helped pave the way for later decisions protecting reproductive rights, including the right to abortion. However, she also contends that conservative extremists are working to block access to birth control and to roll back the legal protections guaranteed in* Griswold. *Borg is director of membership at Population Connection, an environmental organization.*

In 1961 Estelle Griswold, the wife of an Episcopal minister, and Dr. Lee Buxton, a licensed physician and a professor at Yale Medical School, were arrested, tried and convicted as accessories in crime.

Their offense? Providing information, instruction and medical advice on contraception to married couples.

Their conviction stood until June 7, 1965, . . . when the Supreme Court ruled in *Griswold v. Connecticut* that laws prohibiting people from using contraception or counseling others about it violate the constitutional right to privacy.

As a law student, I closely studied *Griswold v. Connecticut* and how it profoundly deepened the constitutional right of individuals to be free from government intrusion in their own private lives.

But most Americans know little about this landmark case that first affirmed our right to use modern birth control and has served as the legal foundation for rulings on sexual relations, reproductive rights and family life ever since.

States Dictated Sexual Relations

For most of the 20th century, a majority of state governments dictated the nature of sexual relations of Americans by denying them the ability to plan their families.

In the early 1960s, laws in 28 states made it illegal for married couples to use contraception. That finally changed when the Supreme Court ruled 7-2 in *Griswold v. Connecticut* that the statute prohibiting the use of contraceptives violated the right of marital privacy.

The precedent set by *Griswold* established the legal basis for extending the right to privacy to non-married individuals in 1972 [in *Eisenstadt v. Baird]* and affirming the right to abortion in *Roe v. Wade.*

In the 40 years since this groundbreaking decision, birth control has become the most commonly used drug among American women in their childbearing years. And our right to birth control is something nearly everyone takes for granted.

Our nation took a great step forward by recognizing the right of individuals to make their own private decisions about planning their families. *Griswold* also set the stage for the beginning of the progressive movement to stabilize world population. By allowing couples to decide the number and spacing of their children, the ruling helped to slow population growth based on personal choice, not government fiat.

But, sadly, Americans' right to birth control is increasingly threatened.

Some ideologues have long wanted to deny women this important tool and bring America back to the days when Estelle Griswold was arrested.

Senator Rick Santorum and Representative Tom Delay have both recently suggested that Americans have no real right to privacy.

For example, Santorum said that he thought states should have the power to outlaw birth control. And he's the third-highest-ranking member of the U.S. Senate.

Griswold (second from left) and Buxton (right) were arrested and put on trial for violating Connecticut's anti–birth control laws. The Supreme Court reversed the convictions and invalidated the law in 1965. © Bettmann/CORBIS

Obstacles to Family Planning

The radical right is doing everything in their power to block access to family planning. The average American woman, who spends 30 years of her life trying to prevent unwanted pregnancy, has to contend with several serious obstacles:

- The FDA [Food and Drug Administration] is stalling on the second application for over-the-counter access for the emergency contraceptive Plan B, despite the fact that their own advisory panel has advocated for such availability.

- The cost of contraception prevents many women from fulfilling their family planning needs. Even if a woman has health insurance, her plan may not cover birth control. Title X—the national family planning program that offers publicly supported contraceptive care to low income and uninsured women—needs more funding to serve an increasing uninsured population.

- At the urging of right-wing political leadership, a growing number of pharmacists around the country are now refusing to fill prescriptions for birth control. [As of 2005] four states have laws or regulations that give legal cover to pharmacists who refuse to fill prescriptions and legislatures in 13 states have introduced measures to do the same.

- Fewer young people are now learning about contraception at school. The federal government is currently [2005] spending millions each year to teach abstinence-only curricula. These programs mention contraception only in terms of failure rates, which are often grossly exaggerated and factually inaccurate.

Right-wing extremists, led by President [George W.] Bush and high-ranking congressional leadership, want to take away our right to birth control. It's time to fight back. In a country where half of all pregnancies are unwanted or mistimed, access to contraception should be expanded, not curtailed.

As we commemorate the 40th anniversary of *Griswold v. Connecticut* we must work harder than ever to ensure that all Americans can exercise their right to privacy and plan their families according to their own very personal decisions.

CHAPTER 3

Legalizing Abortion

Case Overview

Roe v. Wade (1973)

In the landmark case of *Roe v. Wade* the U.S. Supreme Court held that pregnant women had a constitutional right to obtain an abortion free of government interference, at least through the early months of the pregnancy. The decision overturned state laws against abortion. It has been controversial ever since.

The legal case began in 1970 when Texas attorneys Sarah Weddington and Linda Coffee filed a lawsuit challenging a Texas law banning all abortions except those necessary to save a mother's life. The suit was filed on behalf of "Jane Roe" (years later identified as Norma McCorvey), a young, unmarried pregnant woman who had agreed to become the plaintiff in this class-action case. The named defendant was Texas District Attorney Henry B. Wade.

Arguments were first made in May 1970 before the Fifth Circuit Court in Dallas, Texas. Roe's lawyers contended that the Texas abortion law deprived Roe of rights found in the Ninth and Fourteenth Amendments to the U.S. Constitution. Jay Floyd, arguing for the state, contended that "the right of the child to life is superior to that woman's right to privacy." The three-judge panel ruled in June 1970 that the Texas abortion law was unconstitutional. However, it did not order Texas to end its enforcement of the law, enabling Weddington and Coffee to appeal the case directly to the Supreme Court. The case was actually argued before the Court twice—once in December 1971 (when the Court had only seven sitting justices) and again in October 1972. By that time Roe herself had already given birth.

The Supreme Court's 7-2 decision overturning the laws of Texas and other states banning abortion was based on several arguments. It said that state abortion laws aimed at protecting a woman's health were no longer necessary because advances in technology had made abortion safer than childbirth. In addition, the Court found that the right to privacy established by the 1965 *Griswold v. Connecticut* case involving contraceptives was broad enough to encompass a woman's decision to terminate her pregnancy (prior to the fetus's viability). Finally, the Court concluded that fetuses did not constitute "persons" under the Fourteenth Amendment. *Roe* established a trimester framework. During the first trimester (the first three months of a woman's pregnancy), abortion was to be unregulated by law. During the second trimester, states could regulate abortion in ways necessary to protect a woman's health. During the third trimester, after the fetus is deemed "viable," or able to survive outside the womb, states would be permitted to regulate or restrict abortion except when necessary to preserve a woman's life.

Roe v. Wade has engendered political controversy ever since its announcement, creating a divide between "pro-choice" advocates, who believe that the ability to end an unwanted pregnancy is a fundamental reproductive right, and "pro-life" advocates, who believe that destroying a fetus is tantamount to murder. (In an ironic twist, Norma McCorvey, aka Jane Roe, became a spokesperson for pro-choice organizations only to later have a change of heart and become a prominent antiabortion activist.) The issue of abortion has been contested in more than twenty Supreme Court decisions since 1973. The Supreme Court has moved away somewhat from the trimester framework posited in *Roe* and has upheld various government regulations and restrictions on abortion, but it has continued to reaffirm the view that abortion is a basic human right, maintaining that abortion restrictions should never place an "undue burden" on women.

| "We ... conclude that the right of personal privacy
| includes the abortion decision."

The Court's Decision: The Right to Privacy Includes a Right to Abortion

Harry Blackmun

Harry Blackmun served as an associate justice of the Supreme Court from 1970 to 1994. The following selection consists of excerpts from perhaps his most famous legal writing: The majority opinion in the 1973 case of Roe v. Wade. *That landmark decision extended a woman's constitutional right to privacy—first established in* Griswold v. Connecticut—*to encompass a right to choose abortion. Blackmun's opinion, which includes a medical and legal history of abortion practices and laws in the United States and other countries, reflects his background as legal counsel to the Mayo Clinic in Minnesota. Blackmun contends that most abortion laws were designed to protect a woman's health—a rationale that no longer exists because of medical advances. He also argues that an unborn fetus should not be considered a "person" with constitutional rights. The associate justice establishes a trimester framework that empowers state governments to enact greater restrictions on abortions in later stages of pregnancy.*

This Texas federal appeal and its Georgia companion, *Doe v. Bolton,* present constitutional challenges to state criminal abortion legislation. The Texas statutes under attack here are typical of those that have been in effect in many States for approximately a century. . . .

Harry Blackmun, majority opinion, *Roe v. Wade,* 1973.

We forthwith acknowledge our awareness of the sensitive and emotional nature of the abortion controversy, of the vigorous opposing views, even among physicians, and of the deep and seemingly absolute convictions that the subject inspires. One's philosophy, one's experiences, one's exposure to the raw edges of human existence, one's religious training, one's attitudes toward life and family and their values, and the moral standards one establishes and seeks to observe, are all likely to influence and to color one's thinking and conclusions about abortion. . . .

Our task, of course, is to resolve the issue by constitutional measurement, free of emotion and of predilection. We seek earnestly to do this, and, because we do, we have inquired into, and in this opinion place some emphasis upon, medical and medical-legal history and what that history reveals about man's attitudes toward the abortion procedure over the centuries. We bear in mind, too, Mr. Justice [Oliver Wendell] Holmes' admonition in his now vindicated dissent in *Lochner v. New York*, (1905):

> [The Constitution] is made for people of fundamentally differing views, and the accident of our finding certain opinions natural and familiar or novel and even shocking ought not to conclude our judgment upon the question whether statutes embodying them conflict with the Constitution of the United States.

The Texas statutes that concern us here are Arts. 1191–1194 and 1196 of the State's Penal Code. These make it a crime to "procure an abortion," as therein defined, or to attempt one, except with respect to "an abortion procured or attempted by medical advice for the purpose of saving the life of the mother." Similar statutes are in existence in a majority of the States. . . .

The principal thrust of appellant's attack on the Texas statutes is that they improperly invade a right, said to be possessed by the pregnant woman, to choose to terminate her pregnancy. Appellant would discover this right in the concept of personal "liberty" embodied in the Fourteenth Amendment's Due Process Clause; or in personal, marital, familial, and sexual privacy said to be protected by the Bill of Rights or its penumbras, . . . or among those rights reserved to the people by the Ninth Amendment. . . . Before addressing this claim, we feel it desirable briefly to survey, in several aspects, the history of abortion, for such insight as that history may afford us, and then to examine the state purposes and interests behind the criminal abortion laws.

It perhaps is not generally appreciated that the restrictive criminal abortion laws in effect in a majority of States today are of relatively recent vintage. Those laws, generally proscribing abortion or its attempt at any time during pregnancy except when necessary to preserve the pregnant woman's life, are not of ancient or even of common-law origin. Instead, they derive from statutory changes effected, for the most part, in the latter half of the 19th century.

1. Ancient attitudes. These are not capable of precise determination. We are told that at the time of the Persian Empire abortifacients were known and that criminal abortions were severely punished. We are also told, however, that abortion was practiced in Greek times as well as in the Roman Era. . . . Greek and Roman law afforded little protection to the unborn. If abortion was prosecuted in some places, it seems to have been based on a concept of a violation of the father's right to his offspring. Ancient religion did not bar abortion. . . .

3. The common law. It is undisputed that at common law, abortion performed *before* "quickening"—the first recognizable movement of the fetus *in utero,* appearing usually from the 16th to the 18th week of pregnancy—was not an indictable offense. The absence of a common-law crime for pre-quickening abortion appears to have developed from a confluence of earlier philosophical, theological, and civil and canon law concepts of when life begins. These disciplines variously approached the question in terms of the point at which the embryo or fetus became "formed" or recognizably human, or in terms of when a "person" came into being, that is, infused with a "soul" or "animated." A loose consensus evolved in early English law that these events occurred at some point between conception and live birth. This was "mediate animation." Although Christian theology and the canon law came to fix the point of animation at 40 days for a male and 80 days for a female, a view that persisted until the 19th century, there was otherwise little agreement about the precise time of formation or animation. There was agreement, however, that prior to this point the fetus was to be regarded as part of the mother, and its destruction, therefore, was not homicide. . . .

Whether abortion of a *quick* fetus was a felony at common law, or even a lesser crime, is still disputed. A recent review of the common-law precedents argues, . . . that even post-quickening abortion was never established as a common-law crime. . . .

4. The English statutory law. England's first criminal abortion statute, Lord Ellenborough's Act, came in 1803. It made abortion of a quick fetus, § 1, a capital crime, but in § 2 it provided lesser penalties for the felony of abortion before quickening, and thus preserved the "quickening" distinction. . . .

5. The American law. In this country, the law in effect in all but a few States until mid-19th century was the pre-existing English common law. Connecticut, the first State to enact abortion legislation, adopted in 1821 that part of Lord Ellenborough's Act that related to a woman "quick with child." The death penalty was not imposed. Abortion before quickening was made a crime in that State only in 1860. In 1828, New York enacted legislation that, in two respects, was to serve as a model for early anti-abortion statutes. First, while barring destruction of an unquickened fetus as well as a quick fetus, it made the former only a misdemeanor, but the latter second-degree manslaughter. Second, it incorporated a concept of therapeutic abortion by providing that an abortion was excused if it "shall have been necessary to preserve the life of such mother, or shall have been advised by two physicians to be necessary for such purpose." By 1840, when Texas had received the common law, only eight American States had statutes dealing with abortion. It was not until after the War Between the States that legislation began generally to replace the common law. Most of these initial statutes dealt severely with abortion after quickening but were lenient with it before quickening. Most punished attempts equally with completed abortions. While many statutes included the exception for an abortion thought by one or more physicians to be necessary to save the mother's life, that provision soon disappeared and the typical law required that the procedure actually be necessary for that purpose.

Gradually, in the middle and late 19th century the quickening distinction disappeared from the statutory law of most States and the degree of the offense and the penalties were increased. By the end of the 1950's, a large majority of the jurisdictions banned abortion, however and whenever performed, unless done to save or preserve the life of the mother. The exceptions, Alabama and the District of Columbia, permitted abortion to preserve the mother's health. Three States permitted abortions that were not "unlawfully" performed or that were not "without lawful justification," leaving interpretation of those standards to the courts. In the past several years, however, a trend toward liberalization of abortion statutes has resulted in adoption, by about one-third of the States, of less stringent laws. . . .

It is thus apparent that at common law, at the time of the adoption of our Constitution, and throughout the major portion of the 19th century, abortion was viewed with less disfavor than under most American statutes currently in effect.

Phrasing it another way, a woman enjoyed a substantially broader right to terminate a pregnancy than she does in most States today. At least with respect to the early stage of pregnancy, and very possibly without such a limitation, the opportunity to make this choice was present in this country well into the 19th century. Even later, the law continued for some time to treat less punitively an abortion procured in early pregnancy. . . .

Three reasons have been advanced to explain historically the enactment of criminal abortion laws in the 19th century and to justify their continued existence.

It has been argued occasionally that these laws were the product of a Victorian social concern to discourage illicit sexual conduct. Texas, however, does not advance this justification in the present case, and it appears that no court or commentator has taken the argument seriously. . . .

A second reason is concerned with abortion as a medical procedure. When most criminal abortion laws were first enacted, the procedure was a hazardous one for the woman. This was particularly true prior to the development of antisepsis. Antiseptic techniques . . . were not generally accepted and employed until about the turn of the century. Abortion mortality was high. Even after 1900, and perhaps until as late as the development of antibiotics in the 1940's, standard modern techniques such as dilation and curettage were not nearly so safe as they are today. Thus, it has been argued that a State's real concern in enacting a criminal abortion law was to protect the pregnant woman, that is, to restrain her from submitting to a procedure that placed her life in serious jeopardy.

Modern medical techniques have altered this situation. Appellants . . . refer to medical data indicating that abortion in early pregnancy, that is, prior to the end of the first trimester, although not without its risk, is now relatively safe. Mortality rates for women undergoing early abortions, where the procedure is legal, appear to be as low as or lower than the rates for normal childbirth. Consequently, any interest of the State in protecting the woman from an inherently hazardous procedure, except when it would be equally dangerous for her to forgo it, has largely disappeared. Of course, important state interests in the areas of health and medical standards do remain. The State has a legitimate interest in seeing to it that abortion, like any other medical procedure, is performed under circumstances that insure maximum safety for the patient. This interest obviously extends at least to the performing physician and his staff, to the facilities involved, to the availability of after-care, and to adequate provision for any complication or emergency that might arise. The prevalence of high mortality rates at illegal "abortion mills" strengthens, rather than weakens, the State's interest in regulating the conditions under which abortions are performed. Moreover, the risk to the woman increases as her pregnancy continues. Thus, the State retains a definite interest in protecting the woman's own health and safety when an abortion is proposed at a late stage of pregnancy.

The third reason is the State's interest—some phrase it in terms of duty—in protecting prenatal life. Some of the argument for this justification rests on the theory that a new human life is present from the moment of conception. The State's interest and general obligation to protect life then extends, it is argued, to prenatal life. Only when the life of the pregnant mother herself is at stake, balanced against the life she carries within her, should the interest of the embryo or fetus not prevail. Logically, of course, a legitimate state interest in this area need not stand or fall on acceptance of the belief that life begins at conception or at some other point prior to live birth. In assessing the State's interest, recognition may be given to the less rigid claim that as long as at least *potential* life is involved, the State may assert interests beyond the protection of the pregnant woman alone.

Parties challenging state abortion laws have sharply disputed in some courts the contention that a purpose of these laws, when enacted, was to protect prenatal life. Pointing to the absence of legislative history to support the contention, they claim that most state laws were designed solely to protect the woman. Because medical advances have lessened this concern, at least with respect to abortions in early pregnancy, they argue that with respect to such abortions the laws can no longer be justified by any state interest. There is some scholarly support for this view of original purpose. The few state courts called upon to interpret their laws in the late 19th and early 20th centuries did focus on the State's interest in protecting the woman's health rather than in preserving the embryo and fetus. Proponents of this view point out that in many States, including Texas, by statute or judicial interpretation, the pregnant woman herself could not be prosecuted for self-abortion or for cooperating in an abortion performed upon her by another. They claim that adoption of the "quickening" distinction through received common law and state statutes tacitly recognizes the greater health hazards inherent in late abortion and impliedly repudiates the theory that life begins at conception.

It is with these interests, and the weight to be attached to them, that this case is concerned.

The Constitution does not explicitly mention any right of privacy. In a line of decisions, however, going back perhaps as far as *Union Pacific R. Co. v. Botsford,* (1891), the Court has recognized that a right of personal privacy, or a guarantee of certain areas or zones of privacy, does exist under the Constitution. In varying contexts, the Court or individual Justices have, indeed, found at least the roots of that right in the First Amendment, in the Fourth and Fifth Amendments, in the penumbras of the Bill of Rights, in the Ninth Amendment, or in the concept of liberty guaranteed by the first section of the Fourteenth Amendment. . . .

This right of privacy, whether it be founded in the Fourteenth Amendment's concept of personal liberty and restrictions upon state action, as we feel it is, or, as the District Court determined, in the Ninth Amendment's reservation of rights to the people, is broad enough to encompass a woman's decision whether or not to terminate her pregnancy. The detriment that the State would impose upon the pregnant woman by denying this choice altogether is apparent. Specific and direct harm medically diagnosable even in early pregnancy may be involved. Maternity, or additional offspring, may force upon the woman a distressful life and future. Psychological harm may be imminent. Mental and physical health may be taxed by child care. There is also the distress, for all concerned, associated with the unwanted child, and there is the problem of bringing a child into a family already unable, psychologically and otherwise, to care for it. In other cases, as in this one, the additional difficulties and continuing stigma of unwed motherhood may be involved. All these are factors the woman and her responsible physician necessarily will consider in consultation.

On the basis of elements such as these, appellant and some *amici* [friends of the court] argue that the woman's right is absolute and that she is entitled to terminate her pregnancy at whatever time, in whatever way, and for whatever reason she alone chooses. With this we do not agree. Appellant's arguments that Texas either has no valid interest at all in regulating the abortion decision, or no interest strong enough to support any limitation upon the woman's sole determination, are unpersuasive. The Court's decisions recognizing a right of privacy also acknowledge that some state regulation in areas protected by that right is appropriate. As noted above, a State may properly assert important interests in safeguarding health, in maintaining medical standards, and in protecting potential life. At some point in pregnancy, these respective interests become sufficiently compelling to sustain regulation of the factors that govern the abortion decision. The privacy right involved, therefore, cannot be said to be absolute. In fact, it is not clear to us that the claim asserted by some *amici* that one has an unlimited right to do with one's body as one pleases bears a close relationship to the right of privacy previously articulated in the Court's decisions. The Court has refused to recognize an unlimited right of this kind in the past. *Jacobson v. Massachusetts,* (1905) (vaccination); *Buck v. Bell,* (1927) (sterilization).

We, therefore, conclude that the right of personal privacy includes the abortion decision, but that this right is not unqualified and must be considered against important state interests in regulation. . . .

Is the Fetus a Person?

The appellee and certain *amici* argue that the fetus is a "person" within the language and meaning of the Fourteenth Amendment. In support of this, they outline at length and in detail the well-known facts of fetal development. If this suggestion of personhood is established, the appellant's case, of course, collapses, for the fetus' right to life would then be guaranteed specifically by the Amendment. . . .

The Constitution does not define "person" in so many words. Section 1 of the Fourteenth Amendment contains three references to "person." The first, in defining "citizens," speaks of "persons born or naturalized in the United States." The word also appears both in the Due Process Clause and in the Equal Protection Clause. "Person" is used in other places in the Constitution. . . . But in nearly all these instances, the use of the word is such that it has application only postnatally. None indicates, with any assurance, that it has any possible prenatal application.

All this, together with our observation . . . that throughout the major portion of the 19th century prevailing legal abortion practices were far freer than they are today, persuades us

that the word "person," as used in the Fourteenth Amendment, does not include the unborn. . . .

When Does Life Begin?

Texas urges that, apart from the Fourteenth Amendment, life
begins at conception and is present throughout pregnancy,
and that, therefore, the State has a compelling interest in protecting that life from and after conception. We need not resolve the difficult question of when life begins. When those
trained in the respective disciplines of medicine, philosophy,
and theology are unable to arrive at any consensus, the judiciary, at this point in the development of man's knowledge, is
not in a position to speculate as to the answer.

It should be sufficient to note briefly the wide divergence
of thinking on this most sensitive and difficult question. There
has always been strong support for the view that life does not
begin until live birth. This was the belief of the Stoics. It appears to be the predominant, though not the unanimous, atti-
tude of the Jewish faith. It may be taken to represent also the
position of a large segment of the Protestant community, in-
sofar as that can be ascertained; organized groups that have
taken a formal position on the abortion issue have generally
regarded abortion as a matter for the conscience of the individual and her family. As we have noted, the common law
found greater significance in quickening. Physicians and their
scientific colleagues have regarded that event with less interest
and have tended to focus either upon conception, upon live
birth, or upon the interim point at which the fetus becomes
"viable," that is, potentially able to live outside the mother's
womb, albeit with artificial aid. Viability is usually placed at
about seven months (28 weeks) but may occur earlier, even at
24 weeks. The Aristotelian theory of "mediate animation," that
held sway throughout the Middle Ages and the Renaissance in
Europe, continued to be official Roman Catholic dogma until
the 19th century, despite opposition to this "ensoulment"

theory from those in the Church who would recognize the existence of life from the moment of conception. The latter is now, of course, the official belief of the Catholic Church. . . . This is a view strongly held by many non-Catholics as well, and by many physicians.

In areas other than criminal abortion, the law has been reluctant to endorse any theory that life, as we recognize it, begins before live birth or to accord legal rights to the unborn except in narrowly defined situations and except when the rights are contingent upon live birth. . . .

State Interests

In view of all this, we do not agree that, by adopting one theory of life, Texas may override the rights of the pregnant woman that are at stake. We repeat, however, that the State does have an important and legitimate interest in preserving and protecting the health of the pregnant woman, whether she be a resident of the State or a nonresident who seeks medical consultation and treatment there, and that it has still *another* important and legitimate interest in protecting the potentiality of human life. These interests are separate and distinct. Each grows in substantiality as the woman approaches term and, at a point during pregnancy, each becomes "compelling."

With respect to the State's important and legitimate interest in the health of the mother, the "compelling" point, in the light of present medical knowledge, is at approximately the end of the first trimester. This is so because of the now-established medical fact . . . that until the end of the first trimester mortality in abortion may be less than mortality in normal childbirth. It follows that, from and after this point, a State may regulate the abortion procedure to the extent that the regulation reasonably relates to the preservation and protection of maternal health. Examples of permissible state regulation in this area are requirements as to the qualifications of the person who is to perform the abortion; as to the licensure of that person; as to the facility in which the procedure is to be performed, that is, whether it must be a hospital or may be a clinic or some other place of less-than-hospital status; as to the licensing of the facility; and the like.

This means, on the other hand, that, for the period of pregnancy prior to this "compelling" point, the attending physician, in consultation with his patient, is free to determine, without regulation by the State, that, in his medical judgment, the patient's pregnancy should be terminated. If that decision is reached, the judgment may be effectuated by an abortion free of interference by the State.

With respect to the State's important and legitimate interest in potential life, the "compelling" point is at viability. This is so because the fetus then presumably has the capability of meaningful life outside the mother's womb. State regulation protective of fetal life after viability thus has both logical and biological justifications. If the State is interested in protecting fetal life after viability, it may go so far as to proscribe abortion during that period, except when it is necessary to preserve the life or health of the mother.

Measured against these standards, Art. 1196 of the Texas Penal Code, in restricting legal abortions to those "procured or attempted by medical advice for the purpose of saving the life of the mother," sweeps too broadly. The statute makes no distinction between abortions performed early in pregnancy and those performed later, and it limits to a single reason, "saving" the mother's life, the legal justification for the procedure. The statute, therefore, cannot survive the constitutional attack made upon it here. . . .

A Summary

To summarize and to repeat:

1. A state criminal abortion statute of the current Texas type, that excepts from criminality only a *life-saving* proce-

dure on behalf of the mother, without regard to pregnancy stage and without recognition of the other interests involved, is violative of the Due Process Clause of the Fourteenth Amendment.

(a) For the stage prior to approximately the end of the first trimester, the abortion decision and its effectuation must be left to the medical judgment of the pregnant woman's attending physician.

(b) For the stage subsequent to approximately the end of the first trimester, the State, in promoting its interest in the health of the mother, may, if it chooses, regulate the abortion procedure in ways that are reasonably related to maternal health.

(c) For the stage subsequent to viability, the State in promoting its interest in the potentiality of human life may, if it chooses, regulate, and even proscribe, abortion except where it is necessary, in appropriate medical judgment, for the preservation of the life or health of the mother. . . .

This holding, we feel, is consistent with the relative weights of the respective interests involved, with the lessons and examples of medical and legal history, with the lenity of the common law, and with the demands of the profound problems of the present day.

> "The Court apparently values the convenience of the pregnant mother more than the continued existence and development of the life or potential life that she carries."

Dissenting Opinion: There Is No Constitutional Right to Abortion

Bryon R. White

Bryon R. White served as an associate justice for the U.S. Supreme Court from 1962 to 1993. He was one of two dissenting justices in the 1973 case of Roe v. Wade *that legalized abortion in the United States. The following is taken from his dissenting opinion in* Roe *(it also applied to* Doe v. Bolton, *a related case challenging state abortion laws that was decided the same day as* Roe*). White criticizes the majority's legalization of abortion as an unjustified "exercise of raw judicial power" and argues that there is nothing in the Constitution that suggests that women have the right to an abortion. Abortion policy should be decided by the people and their elected political representatives, he concludes.*

At the heart of the controversy . . . are those recurring pregnancies that pose no danger whatsoever to the life or health of the mother but are, nevertheless, unwanted for any one or more of a variety of reasons—convenience, family planning, economics, dislike of children, the embarrassment of illegitimacy, etc. The common claim before us is that for any one of such reasons, or for no reason at all, and without

Bryon R. White, dissenting opinion, *Roe v. Wade,* 1973.

asserting or claiming any threat to life or health, any woman is entitled to an abortion at her request if she is able to find a medical advisor willing to undertake the procedure.

The Court for the most part sustains this position: During the period prior to the time the fetus becomes viable, the Constitution of the United States values the convenience, whim, or caprice of the putative mother more than the life or potential life of the fetus; the Constitution, therefore, guarantees the right to an abortion as against any state law or policy seeking to protect the fetus from an abortion not prompted by more compelling reasons of the mother.

An Exercise of Raw Judicial Power

With all due respect, I dissent. I find nothing in the language or history of the Constitution to support the Court's judgment. The Court simply fashions and announces a new constitutional right for pregnant mothers and, with scarcely any reason or authority for its action, invests that right with sufficient substance to override most existing state abortion statutes. The upshot is that the people and the legislatures of the 50 States are constitutionally disentitled to weigh the relative importance of the continued existence and development of the fetus, on the one hand, against a spectrum of possible impacts on the mother, on the other hand. As an exercise of raw judicial power, the Court perhaps has authority to do what it does today; but in my view its judgment is an improvident and extravagant exercise of the power of judicial review that the Constitution extends to this Court.

The Court apparently values the convenience of the pregnant mother more than the continued existence and development of the life or potential life that she carries. Whether or not I might agree with the marshaling of values, I can in no event join the Court's judgment because I find no constitutional warrant for imposing such an order of priorities on the people and legislatures of the States. In a sensitive area such as this, involving as it does issues over which reasonable men may easily and heatedly differ, I cannot accept the Court's exercise of its clear power of choice by interposing a constitutional barrier to state efforts to protect human life and by investing mothers and doctors with the constitutionally protected right to exterminate it. This issue, for the most part, should be left with the people and to the political processes the people have devised to govern their affairs.

*"The reverberations of the Court's monu-
mental ruling were felt in doctor's offices
and hospital hallways."*

Abortion: What Happens Now?

Matt Clark

The following selection is taken from a 1973 article in Newsweek *magazine immediately following the announcement that
the Supreme Court had overturned most state laws restricting
abortion, concluding that such laws violated a person's constitutional right to privacy. Matt Clark, medical editor for the magazine, examines how the ruling will affect women as well as the
practices of hospitals. Among other predictions, he believes prices
for abortions will drop and that fewer women will travel to
other states to obtain them.*

One day last week, a pregnant 20-year-old Wayne State
University coed visited the offices of a Detroit agency to
arrange for an abortion. Such operations were illegal in Michi-
gan except to protect the life of the mother, so for $200 the
agency would fly her to a clinic in Buffalo, N.Y., where abortion on demand has been available since 1970. But as soon as
she walked in the door, the young woman received some surprising news. Because the U.S. Supreme Court had just overturned all restrictive state abortion laws, she could receive her
abortion that very day in the offices of a Detroit physician.

So it went across the U.S. last week as the reverberations
of the Court's monumental ruling were felt in doctor's offices
and hospital hallways. Inquiries from women seeking abor-

tions swamped the switchboard at Chicago's sprawling Cook County Hospital. In Beverly Hills, a respected gynecologist, who had been violating California law by doing abortions in his office, drank a cold-duck toast over a newly arrived vacuum extraction device with which he would perform his first legal abortion in two years. At Planned Parenthood-World Population in New York, staffers made plans to help establish nonprofit clinics in 40 states, all linked by a toll-free nation-wide telephone referral system.

In its sweeping decision, the Supreme Court ruled that abortions in the first three months of pregnancy are a matter to be decided upon by a woman and her doctor and not sub-ject to any scrutiny by the state. The decision thus voided re-strictive laws in 31 states that permit abortions only to save the life of the mother; it also requires revision of "liberalized" laws in fifteen states that permit abortions, subject to qualifi-cations. (In the remaining four states, abortion on demand is already the law.) In many areas, however, it may be some time before the decision is felt. "We're waiting to see what our legal counsel advises," says a spokesman for a suburban Atlanta hospital where only a dozen abortions were done last year, "and we're sure our legal counsel will proceed slowly."

Most lawyers active in the abortion field think that the Su-preme Court decision makes it incumbent on municipal and public hospitals that have obstetrical facilities to make them available for abortions. "But you can bet," says Lawrence Lader, director of the National Association for the Repeal of Abor-tion Laws, "that we're going to have trouble when it comes to heavily Catholic areas."

Funds

Even Catholic hospitals, which do not now permit abortions, may begin to feel pressure, particularly in rural areas where they may be the only institutions with obstetrical facilities. A precedent may already have been set in Billings, Mont. There,

St. Vincent's Hospital is under a temporary injunction pending the outcome of a case in Federal court to permit sterilization procedures in violation of Catholic doctrine. In imposing the injunction, the court noted that the hospital had once received Federal funds and also that it was the only area hospital with a maternity service.

Hospital policies against abortion may not, however, prove decisive in the long run toward determining the availability of abortions, since the Supreme Court decision clearly permits such operations to be done in the doctor's office in the first trimester. "If we find an area where hospitals legitimately refuse to perform abortions," says Lader, "then we'll have to get doctors who will perform them on their own."

Some pro-abortion physicians are concerned about the Supreme Court's green light for office abortions. "It's possible with this ruling," says Dr. John Marshall, chief of obstetrics and gynecology at Harbor General Hospital in Torrance, Calif., "that every Tom, Dick and Harry out in the woods can start doing abortions and we'll be back where we were before abortion was legal."

Quick

Some observers believe the decision will even permit abortions by paramedical personnel, working under the supervision of a doctor. Harvey Karmen, a Los Angeles clinical psychologist who has been arrested numerous times for performing abortions, announced last week that he had found a physician who would act as his backup. Karmen has already trained some 60 lay women in the use of the Karmen cannula, a simple device he has invented for performing quick abortions by suction.

In an effort to eliminate the potential hazards of office abortions, NARAL [National Abortion Rights Action League] and Planned Parenthood plan to run seminars around the country on how to set up outpatient abortion clinics like

those in New York City. There strict regulations have produced a remarkable safety record: there have been no abortion
deaths in New York City since July 1971. Many of the clinics,
such as one about to open at Harbor General, will offer abortions as part of a comprehensive family-planning service that
includes advice on contraception. "If a woman comes into the
office and all you do is empty her womb, all you've treated is
the symptom," notes Marshall. "You have to treat the disease—irresponsible sexuality—as well."

With clinics and in-office procedures, the price of abortions will undoubtedly come down. An abortion in some hospitals currently costs about $400 to $600, even in the first trimester. Outpatient clinic abortions cost as little as $100.

Another of the positive results of last week's decision,
some observers think, will be to put profitmaking abortion-
referral entrepreneurs out of business. One such operator,
Henry Dubin, made $100,000 last year, acting as business
agent for at least five Los Angeles-area hospitals which offer
abortions (NEWSWEEK, Nov. 13, 1972). Members of the radical
Feminist Women's Health Center in Los Angeles have been
getting $50 in return for referrals.

Profit

"The handwriting is on the wall," admits Wayne Lamont, director of an Orange County, Calif., referral service. Lamont
believes, however, that he can stay in business by insuring that
he steers women to good hospitals offering safe abortions at
reasonable cost. But California State Sen. Anthony Beilenson
plans to introduce legislation to prohibit abortion referral for
a profit, on the ground that "referral belongs in abortion no
more than in tonsillectomies."

Finally, as abortions become increasingly available across
the country, the need for women to travel far and wide to
states with liberal laws will disappear. At least two-thirds of
the abortions performed in New York City involve out-of-state

women. Until now, Dr. James Ham of the Garberson Clinic in Mile City, Mont., has been referring eight to ten women a month to California and Washington for abortions. "What has been happening," says Ham, "is that if you can afford it you get an abortion, and if you can't you have the child and go on welfare. The decision will be more fair to the individuals and also to the states that have had to take the brunt."

> *"The greatest advance in women's health*
> *in the last half of the twentieth century*
> *... happened in the Supreme Court in*
> *1973."*

Roe Marked a Great Advance in Women's Rights

Melanie Thernstrom

For this article, published in 2003 on the thirtieth anniversary of Roe v. Wade, *freelance writer Melanie Thernstrom interviewed several doctors and abortion providers who had firsthand experience both before and after the 1973 Supreme Court decision. Prior to* Roe, *Thernstorm writes, women facing unwanted pregnancies often risked their lives in seeking illegal abortions, which were often expensive, difficult to obtain, and dangerous. Abortions were often performed by people who had lost (or had never had) medical licenses. Licensed doctors who attempted to work around laws and hospital rules to provide abortions did so at risk to their careers. The Supreme Court decision making abortion legal marked a great advance both for reproductive rights and for women's health, Thernstrom concludes.*

Mildred "Millie" Hanson, M.D., a petite, grandmotherly ob-gyn in Minnesota, has been providing elective abortions since the moment they became legal in 1973. Whenever she gets weary of the protesters, hate mail and death threats, she thinks about a telling memento she has kept through the years: a copy of a death certificate from 1934.

The document takes Dr. Hanson back to her childhood in Wisconsin. A young Catholic neighbor had become pregnant with her seventh child, and because the family was facing the hard times of the Depression, the woman begged her doctor to "do something." He did, but later the woman developed a high fever. Delirious, she convulsed in pain and chewed her lips until they bled. Her husband pleaded with the doctor to hospitalize her, but he refused, fearing authorities would investigate and take away his license. Three days after her abortion, the woman died.

Dr. Hanson, who went to high school with two of the children the woman left behind, later became an obstetrician. Unsettled by the tragedy, she went to the local courthouse and was stunned by what she found. While the vast majority of deaths from botched abortions were falsely attributed to other causes, in her neighbor's case, the cause of death had been accurately stated: "Abortion."

Dr. Hanson took a copy of that certificate with her and embarked upon a lifelong campaign to promote safe, legal abortions and open access to contraception, including 30 years as the medical director of Planned Parenthood of Minnesota/South Dakota. "When you talk about the abortion deaths that occurred [before the Supreme Court handed down the *Roe v. Wade* decision in 1973], young people don't believe it. Young *doctors* don't believe it." she says. "I worry that people who have never seen the horror of illegal abortion are going to allow abortion to become outlawed or very difficult to get."

For women who don't know life before *Roe v. Wade,* the lurid days of backstreet butchers and self-mutilating coathanger abortions can seem as foreign as the use of a scarlet letter to punish adultery. The basic right of women to determine—through contraception and abortion—when and how many times they will bear children has become so integral to the advancement of women's equality in our country that we can hardly imagine life without it. But for doctors who began practicing before 1973, the traumas of that time remain vivid. "The greatest advance in women's health in the last half of the twentieth century didn't happen in the operating room or the lab; it happened in the Supreme Court in 1973," says William Harrison, M.D., an ob-gyn who has practiced in Fayetteville, Arkansas, since 1972. How can one case be so pivotal? Read these stories from doctors who remember that time—and still practice today—and you'll know why we need to protect this right now more than ever.

Abortions Before *Roe v. Wade*

Each of the physicians *Glamour* interviewed recalls a galvanizing case through which he or she first realized how critical access to abortion is to women's health. For Dr. Harrison that case came in 1967, when an impoverished, single mother of many arrived at the hospital where he was a medical student and complained of a swollen abdomen. When he and the resident gave her the diagnosis of pregnancy, she said, "I was hoping it was cancer."

At the time, Dr. Harrison considered himself pro-life. "My wife was pregnant with our third child" he says. "But when I juxtaposed our joy with this woman's despair, I realized there was something about abortion I didn't understand. I've seen her desperation thousands of times, and her case continues to spark my resolution to do abortions."

Steve Tamis, M.D., an ob-gyn in Phoenix, knew abortion was an essential right when, in the early sixties, he delivered the baby of a 16-year-old who had been gang-raped at her prom. While in labor, she kept screaming about how the perpetrators had gone to jail for only six months. "What about *her* sentence?" Dr. Tamis remembers thinking. "For nine months, she was forced to carry a child against her will."

Many women who'd had botched abortions were treated like criminals first, patients second. In 1958, during his residency in Albany, New York, James Armstrong Sr., M.D., a family physician now practicing in Kalispell, Montana, recalls the night when a young woman was admitted to the hospital with an undiagnosed illness; she eventually confessed that she'd had an illegal abortion. "We realized she'd developed septicemia, an overwhelming infection. By law, we had to report that," he remembers. The next day, two male detectives brutally interrogated the woman; a few hours later, she died. After learning how many women had similar complications. Dr. Armstrong says, "There wasn't any question in my mind that abortion had to be legalized."

For Christopher Dotson, M.D., an ob-gyn in Los Angeles who has been practicing since 1963, the painful awakening was personal: While he was an undergraduate in the early fifties, his cousin died of a severe infection caused by an illegal abortion in a small town in Alabama. Later, when Dr. Dotson was a resident at Kings County Hospital Center in Brooklyn, New York, each morning he'd see lines of women in the emergency room who'd had illegal abortions the night before. As he fought to save these women's lives, he says, "I'd think how if my cousin had been one of them, we could have helped her." It was so frustrating to see the ravaging effects of botched abortions, Dr. Dotson says, because "we could have provided adequate medical care in the first place."

Dangerous and Expensive

Two thirds of Americans are in favor of open access to abortions. (And 43 percent of American women will have *had* an abortion by age 45, according to the Kaiser Family Foundation.) Today, the procedure is so safe that of the more than one million abortions performed each year, only a handful result in death. In fact, abortion now has a far lower incidence of maternal mortality than pregnancy. But before *Roe,* when an estimated 200,000 to 1.2 million illegal abortions were performed annually, up to 10,000 women died from them *each year* in the United States, according to the Center for Reproductive Law and Policy in New York City. "Abortion is such an easy, safe way to terminate unwanted pregnancies," says Dr.

A woman protests the closing of an abortion clinic in 1971. Prior to the Roe *ruling in 1973, women facing unwanted pregnancies often risked their lives seeking illegal abortions.* AP/ Wide World Photos

Hanson. "Yet women were dying for lack of safe abortions."

And illegal abortions were tremendously expensive. In the 1950s, the going rate for an abortion in New York City was about $500—the equivalent of about $4,000 today—recalls Dr. Armstrong. Some women were so desperate that they'd nearly starve themselves just to save the money. Those who could scrape together the cash found that it bought them sub-standard care. Illegal-abortion doctors (and sometimes the women themselves) were known to use knitting needles, cro-chet hooks, parts of coat hangers and other crude materials that did awful damage to the women's bodies. The result? Runaway infections. "Women would come to the emergency room in shock or with high fevers," Dr. Hanson says. Those who survived were often left with pelvic infections and infer-tility, which denied them the opportunity to have children when they wanted to.

How could a simple procedure be so dangerous? Many illegal abortionists were carpetbagger entrepreneurs with no medical experience; some had medical training but had lost their licenses due to malpractice, says Dr. Hanson. "I never knew who really performed these abortions," she says. "But they knew me. I developed a reputation as a doctor willing to treat patients with complications from botched abortions." In some cases, illegal abortionists even *relied* on doctors like Dr. Hanson—it meant they didn't have to finish the job. They'd insert something into the woman's uterus (part of a hanger, for example) and send her home. If she started hemorrhaging, she'd go to an emergency room or find a sympathetic doctor like Dr. Hanson, who would use the bleeding as a reason to complete the abortion.

Even that carried great risks for doctors. In the hospital where Dr. Hanson worked, if a doctor performed a D&C (a procedure in which a woman's uterus is emptied) on the grounds that the patient had suffered an incomplete miscarriage, a group called the Tissue Committee would examine the records—even the tissue itself—for evidence that there had been bleeding before the procedure. "If there hadn't been, you'd have some explaining to do," says Dr. Hanson. She didn't proceed without such proof; as a divorced mother of four, she couldn't risk losing her practice or license and serving a prison sentence.

Working Around the Rules

Other doctors tried to work around the laws and strict hospital rules. While in medical school in 1956, Dr. Armstrong had a professor who said a woman in her forties needed a hysterectomy because she had a uterine fibroid. During the procedure, Dr. Armstrong asked him. "Is this how a fibroid feels?" The professor said nothing, but later Dr. Armstrong checked the lab results and found that the uterus contained a 14-to-15-week pregnancy. Neither doctor spoke of it again.

Dr. Tamis was persuaded to provide abortions by an unlikely party: a rabbi who confided that he was a member of the clergymen's underground, a network of religious elders who brought women in need of abortions to trusted doctors. It was the late sixties, and in some states abortions could be performed legally if two physicians certified that the pregnancy was a threat to the woman's life; some women were willing to declare themselves suicidal in order to get the procedure. After discussing it with the rabbi, Dr. Tamis set up a clinic with psychiatrists willing to meet with such desperate women. "It wasn't ideal—a suicide threat became a permanent part of the women's medical records—but many felt this was their only option," he says.

We Can't Go Back

By 1970, Jane Hodgson, M.D., who began practicing in Minnesota in 1947, had seen more than two decades of abortion-related health tragedies. So when a pregnant woman came to her with rubella, a virus that carries up to a 60 percent risk of birth defects or miscarriage when contracted early in pregnancy, Dr. Hodgson decided to take a drastic step: She performed the abortion openly, even publicizing the procedure. "We were all so elated that New York State had just passed a law legalizing abortion—it spurred me on," she says. "I was tired of seeing so many women suffer." Dr. Hodgson was indicted and convicted of performing an illegal abortion; her conviction was overturned only when *Roe v. Wade* was handed down by the Supreme Court. "Abortion is nothing but a tragedy for the women who go through it," she says. It's not an easy decision, but "no one would want to see his or her own daughter forced to go through pregnancy like a baby machine, without any choice. How can we go back to a world like that?"

> *"Under* Casey, *state and local laws that favor fetal rights and burden a woman's choice to have abortion are permitted."*

Roe Has Been Weakened by Subsequent Supreme Court Decisions

Center for Reproductive Rights

Roe v. Wade established abortion rights as part of the nation's laws, but it also inspired a political movement and the creation of various organizations committed to limiting the scope of— and ultimately reverse—the decision. Founded in 1992, the Center for Reproductive Rights is one of several organizations that oppose these efforts and seek to make abortion legal and accessible to all women. In the following viewpoint, written in 2003 on the thirtieth anniversary of Roe v. Wade, *the center contends that* Roe *remains an important decision that recognizes a woman's right to choose abortion. However, the writers also argue that subsequent laws and Supreme Court decisions have weakened the fundamental right to choose abortion and have made it easier for state governments to place restrictions on a woman's access to the procedure.*

On January 22, 1973, the United States Supreme Court struck down the State of Texas's criminal abortion laws, finding that the right to decide whether to have a child is a fundamental right guaranteed by the U.S. Constitution. The 7-2 decision in *Roe v. Wade* would have an immediate and profound effect on the lives of American women.

Before *Roe,* it is estimated (by researchers Willard Cates Jr. and Robert W. Rochat) that "between 200,000 and 1.2 million illegally induced abortions occur[red] annually in the United States." As many as 5,000 to 10,000 women died per year following illegal abortions and many others suffered severe physical and psychological injury.

To prevent women from dying or injuring themselves from unsafe, illegal or self-induced abortions, women's advocates spearheaded campaigns to reverse century-old criminal abortion laws in the decades preceding *Roe.* During the 1960s and 1970s, a movement of medical, public health, legal, religious and women's organizations successfully urged one-third of state legislatures to liberalize their abortion statutes.

Roe v. Wade is a landmark decision that recognized that the right to make childbearing choices is central to women's lives and their ability to participate fully and equally in society. Yet, the Supreme Court's decision in *Roe* was far from radical—it was the logical extension of High Court decisions on the right to privacy dating back to the turn of the century. The decision is grounded in the same reasoning that guarantees our right to refuse medical treatment and the freedom to resist government search and seizure. In finding that the constitutional right to privacy encompasses a woman's right to choose whether or not to continue a pregnancy, the High Court continued a long line of decisions recognizing a right of privacy that protects intimate and personal decisions—including those affecting child-rearing, marriage, procreation and the use of contraception—from governmental interference.

The Decision

In its 1973 decision in *Roe,* the Supreme Court recognized that a woman's right to decide whether to continue her pregnancy was protected under the constitutional provisions of individual autonomy and privacy. For the first time, *Roe* placed women's reproductive choice alongside other fundamental rights, such as freedom of speech and freedom of religion, by conferring the highest degree of constitutional protection—"strict scrutiny"—to choice.

Finding a need to balance a woman's right to privacy with the state's interest in protecting potential life, the Supreme Court established a trimester framework for evaluating restrictions on abortion. The Court required the state to justify any interference with the abortion decision by showing that it had a "compelling interest" in doing so. Restrictions on abortions performed before fetal viability, that is, the period before a fetus can live outside a woman's body, were limited to those that narrowly and precisely promoted real maternal health concerns. After the point of viability, the state was free to ban abortion or take other steps to promote its interest in protecting fetal life. Even after that point, however, the state's interest in the viable fetus must yield to the woman's right to have an abortion to protect her health and life.

Immediately following the *Roe* decision, those who did not want to see women participate equally in society were galvanized. The far right initiated a political onslaught that has resulted in numerous state and federal abortion restrictions and contributed to a changed Supreme Court, ideologically bent on eviscerating *Roe*. The right to choose became the target of not only the religious right, but also right-wing politicians and judges who used the *Roe* decision to attack the "judicial activism" of the Supreme Court and its purported failure to adhere to the text of the Constitution and the "original intent" of its framers. This backlash reached its peak during the three terms of Presidents [Ronald] Reagan and [George H.W.] Bush. Beginning in 1983, the U.S. solicitor general routinely urged the Supreme Court, on behalf of the federal government, to overturn *Roe*. In addition, when appointing Supreme Court Justices, Reagan and Bush used opposition to *Roe* as a litmus test. During this twelve-year period, five justices—

[Sandra Day] O'Connor, [Antonin] Scalia, [Anthony M.] Kennedy, [David] Souter, and [Clarence] Thomas—were appointed. Not one of these five, who still constitute a majority on the Court today [January 2003], supports the "strict scrutiny" standard of review established by *Roe*.

The Dismantling of *Roe*

Shortly after the *Roe* decision, state legislatures began passing laws in hopes of creating exceptions to it or opening up areas of law that *Roe* did not directly address. No other right has been frontally attacked and so successfully undermined, and all in the course of two decades—the same two decades that sustained advances in other areas of women's rights, including education and employment.

Teenagers were the first successful target. In 1979 the Court endorsed state laws that required parental consent, as long as they were accompanied by a complicated system whereby minors could assert their privacy rights by requesting a hearing before a state judge on whether they were "mature" or an abortion was in their best interests (*Bellotti v. Baird*).

The next assault on *Roe* was directed at low-income women. In 1980 the Hyde Amendment, which prohibited Medicaid from covering most abortions, was upheld by the Supreme Court by a 5-4 margin (*Harris v. McRae*). The Court abandoned the neutrality required in *Roe*, finding that, for poor women, government could promote childbearing over abortion, so long as it did so by manipulating women through public funding schemes, not criminal laws.

Dissenting in *City of Akron v. Akron Center for Reproductive Health* (1983), Justice O'Connor called for a radical erosion of *Roe* and proposed that a lesser standard of constitutional protection for choice be established, called the "undue burden" standard, in place of the "strict scrutiny" test. By 1989, after the arrival of Justices Kennedy and Scalia and the elevation of William Rehnquist to chief justice, there were no longer five votes to preserve reproductive choice as a fundamental constitutional right. The Court's ruling in *Webster v. Reproductive Health Services* (1989) demonstrated this new reality when five justices expressed hostility toward *Roe* in differing degrees and essentially called for states to pass legislation banning abortion in order to test the law.

Three years later, in *Casey,* the strict judicial scrutiny established in *Roe* was finally abandoned in a plurality opinion of Justices O'Connor, Kennedy and Souter. Although the Court said it was not overturning *Roe's* central premise that abortion is a fundamental right, the *Casey* decision replaced the original "strict scrutiny" standard governing other fundamental rights for the weak and confusing undue burden standard. This opened the door to a host of state and federal criminal restrictions designed to steer women away from abortion and to promote the rights of the fetus throughout pregnancy. Over 300 criminal abortion restrictions have been enacted by legislatures in the past six years alone, none of which would have been constitutional under the original *Roe* decision.

The Four Pillars of *Roe*

The *Roe* opinion was grounded on four constitutional pillars: (1) the decision to have an abortion was accorded the highest level of constitutional protection like any other fundamental constitutional right; (2) the government had to stay neutral; legislatures could not enact laws that pushed women to make one decision or another; (3) in the period before the fetus is viable, the government may restrict abortion only to protect a woman's health; (4) after viability, the government may prohibit abortion, but laws must make exceptions that permit abortion when necessary to protect a woman's health or life.

Only two of the four *Roe* pillars remain today as a result of the Supreme Court's 1992 decision in *Planned Parenthood of Southeastern Pennsylvania v. Casey.* This decision is the culmination of a steady decline in constitutional protection for the right to privacy. A woman's right to choose is still constitutionally protected, however, the "strict scrutiny" standard was jettisoned in favor of a lesser standard of protection for reproductive choice called "undue burden." Under *Casey,* state and local laws that favor fetal rights and burden a woman's choice to have abortion are permitted, so long as the burden is not "undue." No longer does the state have to be neutral in the choice of abortion or childbearing. Now the government is free to pass laws restricting abortion based on "morality," a code word for religious anti-abortion views. States are now permitted to disfavor abortion and punish women seeking abortions, even those who are young and sick, with harassing laws.

Roe in the 21st Century

In 2000, eight years after the *Casey* decision, the Court agreed to hear another case that opened up *Roe* for reexamination. During that period, President [Bill] Clinton had appointed two justices, (Ruth Bader) Ginsburg and (Stephen) Breyer. The first challenge to *Roe* in the 21st century came in the form of a Nebraska ban on so-called "partial-birth abortion" brought by the Center for Reproductive Rights. The language of the Nebraska ban—and the cookie-cutter versions passed in 30 states—was sweeping and broad, and could have included virtually all abortion procedures, even those used in the early weeks of pregnancy. Publicly, however, supporters of these bans camouflaged this fact by using a term made up by the National Right-to-Life Committee—"partial-birth abortion"—and pretending that the bans were designed to prevent doctors from using one particular procedure.

In a 5-4 vote in the case *Stenberg v. Carhart* (2000), the Court struck down the ban, finding it an unconstitutional violation of *Roe* and *Casey* by failing to include an exception to preserve the health of the woman and by imposing an undue burden on a woman's ability to choose an abortion.

In addition, the Court determined that the effect of the ban went well beyond prohibitions against so-called "late term" abortion, finding the ban to be so broad and vague that constitutionally protected abortion procedures performed before viability could be prohibited. The majority decision was joined by four justices, with four separate dissenting opinions filed by Chief Justice Rehnquist and Justices Scalia, Thomas and Kennedy. Kennedy previously had supported the right to choose abortion in the *Casey* decision.

The 5-4 vote in *Stenberg* is an ominous sign for *Roe*'s future. The Supreme Court is only one vote away from overturning *Roe*, which would be one of the most radical actions taken in the history of the Court. Without *Roe*, life for American women would be thrown more than 30 years in reverse, returning them to the days when women could not fully control the number and spacing of their children. Without the ability to make this key decision, women will be denied opportunities to realize their future and take advantage of educational and career opportunities.

The world is looking to the U.S. to establish a vision of justice for the 21st century. It is not a time for our political leaders to divide this nation by turning the clock back on women's human rights.

> "Like few other Supreme Court cases in
> our nation's history, Roe is not merely
> patently wrong but also fundamentally
> hostile to core precepts of American gov-
> ernment and citizenship."

Roe Is Bad Law and Should Be Reversed

M. Edward Whelan III

*M. Edward Whelan III, a lawyer and former law clerk for Su-
preme Court justice Antonin Scalia, is president of the Ethics
and Public Policy Center, a think tank that promotes the role of
Judeo-Christian traditions in shaping public policy on critical issues. The following selection is taken from testimony before a
Senate subcommittee hearing examining the effects of* Roe v.
Wade. *Whelan argues that* Roe *was a poorly written decision
that imposed a "radical regime of unrestricted abortion" on
America. He also criticizes other Supreme Court decisions affirming the right to abortion. Whelan concludes that the Su-
preme Court should reverse* Roe *and make abortion a matter for
Congress and state legislatures to decide.*

Why are we here today addressing a case that the Supreme Court decided 32 years ago, that it ratified 13
years ago, and that America's cultural elites overwhelmingly
embrace? The answer, I would submit, is twofold.

The *Dred Scott* of Our Age

First, *Roe v. Wade* marks the second time in American history
that the Supreme Court has invoked "substantive due process"

M. Edward Whelan III, testimony before the U.S. Senate Subcommittee on the Constitution, Civil Rights, and Property Rights, Committee on the Judiciary, Washington, DC,
June 23, 2005.

to deny American citizens the authority to protect the basic rights of an entire class of human beings. The first time, of course, was the Court's infamous 1857 decision in the *Dred Scott* case. There, the Court held that the Missouri Compromise of 1820, which prohibited slavery in the northern portion of the Louisiana Territories, could not constitutionally be applied to persons who brought their slaves into free territory. Such a prohibition, the Court nakedly asserted, "could hardly be dignified with the name of due process." Thus were discarded the efforts of the people, through their representatives, to resolve politically and peacefully the greatest moral issue of their age. Chief Justice [Roger] Taney and his concurring colleagues thought that they were conclusively resolving the issue of slavery. Instead, they only made all the more inevitable the Civil War that erupted four years later.

Roe is the *Dred Scott* of our age. Like few other Supreme Court cases in our nation's history, *Roe* is not merely patently wrong but also fundamentally hostile to core precepts of American government and citizenship. *Roe* is a lawless power grab by the Supreme Court, an unconstitutional act of aggression by the Court against the political branches and the American people. *Roe* prevents all Americans from working together, through an ongoing process of peaceful and vigorous persuasion, to establish and revise the policies on abortion governing our respective states. *Roe* imposes on all Americans a radical regime of unrestricted abortion for any reason all the way up to viability—and, under the predominant reading of sloppy language in *Roe*'s companion case, *Doe v. Bolton,* essentially unrestricted even in the period from viability until birth. *Roe* fuels endless litigation in which pro-abortion extremists challenge modest abortion-related measures that state legislators have enacted and that are overwhelmingly favored by the public—provisions, for example, seeking to ensure informed consent and parental involvement for minors and barring atrocities like partial-birth abortion. *Roe* disenfranchises the millions and millions of patriotic American citizens who believe that the self-evident truth proclaimed in the Declaration of Independence—that all men are created equal and are endowed by their Creator with an unalienable right to life—warrants significant governmental protection of the lives of unborn human beings.

So long as Americans remain Americans—so long, that is, as they remain faithful to the foundational principles of this country—I believe that the American body politic will never accept *Roe*.

Clearing the Confusion

The second reason to examine *Roe* is the ongoing confusion that somehow surrounds the decision. Leading political and media figures, deliberately or otherwise, routinely misrepresent and understate the radical nature of the abortion regime that the Court imposed in *Roe*. And, conversely, they distort and exaggerate the consequences of reversing *Roe* and of restoring to the American people the power to determine abortion policy in their respective States. The more that Americans understand *Roe*, the more they regard it as illegitimate.

Reasonable people of good will with differing values or with varying prudential assessments of the practical effect of protective abortion laws may come to a variety of conclusions on what abortion policy ought to be in the many diverse states of this great nation. But, I respectfully submit, it is well past time for all Americans, no matter what their views on abortion, to recognize that the Court-imposed abortion regime should be dismantled and the issue of abortion should be returned to its rightful place in the democratic political process.

Roe v. Wade

In *Roe v. Wade* (1973), the Court addressed the constitutionality of a Texas statute, "typical of those that have been in effect in many States for approximately a century," that made abortion a crime except where "procured or attempted by medical advice for the purpose of saving the life of the mother." The seven-Justice majority, in an opinion by Justice [Harry A.] Blackmun, ruled that the Texas statute violated the Due Process Clause of the Fourteenth Amendment (which provides that no state shall "deprive any person of life, liberty, or property, without due process of law"). The Court ruled that the Due Process Clause requires an abortion regime that comports with these requirements that the Court composed:

"(a) For the stage prior to approximately the end of the first trimester, the abortion decision and its effectuation must be left to the medical judgment of the pregnant woman's attending physician.

"(b) For the stage subsequent to approximately the end of the first trimester, the State, in promoting its interest in the health of the mother, may, if it chooses, regulate the abortion procedure in ways that are reasonably related to maternal health.

"(c) For the stage subsequent to viability, the State in promoting its interest in the potentiality of human life may, if it chooses, regulate, and even proscribe, abortion except where it is necessary, in appropriate medical judgment, for the preservation of the life or health of the mother."

Merely describing *Roe* virtually suffices to refute its legitimacy. One of the two dissenters, Justice Byron White—who was appointed by President Kennedy—accurately observed that Blackmun's opinion was "an exercise of raw judicial power" and "an improvident and extravagant exercise of the power of judicial review." . . .

Doe v. Bolton

The same day that the Court decided *Roe,* it rendered its decision in *Doe v. Bolton* (1973). As the Court said in *Roe, Roe* and *Doe* "are to be read together." *Doe* presented the question whether Georgia's abortion legislation, patterned on the American Law Institute's model legislation, was constitutional. Among other things, the Georgia statute provided that an abortion shall not be criminal when performed by a physician "based upon his best clinical judgment that an abortion is necessary because [a] continuation of the pregnancy would endanger the life of the pregnant woman or would seriously and permanently injure her health." In the course of upholding this provision against a challenge that it was unconstitutionally vague, Justice Blackmun's majority opinion determined that the

> medical judgment [as to health] may be exercised in the light of all factors—physical, emotional, psychological, familial, and the woman's age—relevant to the wellbeing of the patient. All these factors may relate to health. This allows the attending physician the room he needs to make his best medical judgment.

It is not entirely clear what Blackmun's garbled discussion is intended to mean. The predominant assumption appears to be that Blackmun was construing the Georgia statute's health exception in accord with what he regarded as its natural legal meaning (or, alternatively, in a way that he thought necessary to salvage it from invalidation on vagueness grounds). Under this reading, the authority that *Roe* purports to confer on states to "regulate, and even proscribe, abortion" after viability is subject to the loophole of *Doe* 's health exception.... Because the practical meaning of this loophole would appear to be entirely at the discretion of the abortionist, it would swallow any general post-viability prohibition against abortion.

Myths About *Roe*

Myths about *Roe* abound, and I will not strive to dispel all of them here. One set of myths dramatically understates the

Pro-life supporters demonstrate in Washington, D.C., in 2005 during the thirty-second anniversary of the Roe v. Wade *ruling.* Larry Downing/Reuters/Landov

radical nature of the abortion regime that *Roe* invented and imposed on the entire country. *Roe* is often said, for example, merely to have created a constitutional right to abortion during the first three months of pregnancy (or the first trimester). Nothing in *Roe* remotely supports such a characterization.

A more elementary confusion is reflected in the commonplace assertion that *Roe* "legalized" abortion. At one level, this proposition is true, but it completely obscures the fact that the Court did not merely legalize abortion—it *constitutionalized* abortion. In other words, the American people, acting through their state legislators, had the constitutional authority before *Roe* to make abortion policy. (Some States had legalized abortion, and others were in the process of liberalizing their abortion laws.) *Roe* deprived the American people of this authority.

The assertion that *Roe* "legalized" abortion also bears on a surprisingly widespread misunderstanding of the effect of a Supreme Court reversal of *Roe*. Many otherwise well-informed people seem to think that a reversal of *Roe* would mean that abortion would thereby be illegal nationwide. But of course a reversal of *Roe* would merely restore to the people of the States their constitutional authority to establish—and to revise over time—the abortion laws and policies for their respective States.

This confusion about what reversing *Roe* means is also closely related to confusion, or deliberate obfuscation, over what it means for a Supreme Court Justice to be opposed to *Roe*. In particular, such a Justice is often mislabeled "pro-life." But Justices like [William H.] Rehnquist, [Byron R.] White, [Antonin] Scalia, and [Clarence] Thomas, who have recognized that the Constitution does not speak to the question of abortion, take a position that is entirely neutral on the substance of America's abortion laws. Their modest point concerns process: abortion policy is to be made through the political processes, not by the courts. These Justices do not adopt a "pro-life" reading of the Due Process Clause under which permissive abortion laws would themselves be unconstitutional.

Planned Parenthood v. Casey

In 1992, the Supreme Court seemed ready to reverse *Roe* and to end its unconstitutional usurpation of the political processes on the abortion question. Instead, in *Planned Parenthood v. Casey* (1992), Justices [Sandra Day] O'Connor, [Anthony] Kennedy, and [David] Souter combined to produce a joint majority opinion so breathtaking in its grandiose misunderstanding of the Supreme Court's role that it makes one long for the sterile incoherence of Blackmun's opinion in *Roe*. . . .

The core of the Court's explanation of the liberty interests protected by the Due Process Clause is its declaration, "At the heart of liberty is the right to define one's own concept of existence, of meaning, of the universe, and of the mystery of human life." This lofty New Age rhetoric should not conceal the shell game that the Court is playing. What the Court's declaration really means is that the Court is claiming the unconstrained power to define for all Americans which particular interests it thinks should be beyond the bounds of citizens to address through legislation. . . .

While abandoning *Roe*'s trimester framework, the *Casey* joint opinion then reaffirmed what it characterized as *Roe*'s central holding: "a State may not prohibit any woman from making the ultimate decision to terminate her pregnancy before viability." It also stated that it reaffirmed *Roe*'s holding (which, as discussed above, apparently was to be read with *Doe*'s malleable definition of health) that even after viability abortion must be available "where it is necessary, in appropriate medical judgment, for the preservation of the life or health of the mother." In addition, it adopted a subjective and amorphous "undue burden" standard for assessing incidental abortion regulations before viability.

Stenberg v. Carhart

The Supreme Court's decision in 2000 in *Stenberg v. Carhart* provides special insight into the Court's abortion regime. That case presented the question of the constitutionality of Nebraska's ban on partial-birth abortion.

This case crossed my mind five months ago as my daughter was being born and her head was first starting to emerge.

Pardon me as I briefly describe what partial-birth abortion is: It's a method of late-term abortion in which the abortionist dilates the mother's cervix, extracts the baby's body by the feet until all but the head has emerged, stabs a pair of scissors into the head, sucks out the baby's brains, collapses the skull, and delivers the dead baby.

According to estimates cited by the Court, up to 5000 partial-birth abortions are done every year in this much-blessed country.

In the face of a division of opinion among doctors over whether partial-birth abortion is sometimes safer than other methods of abortion, the Court, by a 5-4 vote, deferred to the view of those who maintained that it sometimes is and invalidated the Nebraska statute banning it.

I don't have much else to say about this case. I don't dispute at all that its result can reasonably be thought to be dictated by *Roe* and *Casey*. And I certainly don't contend that what partial-birth abortion yields—a dead baby—is any different from what other methods of abortion yield.

I would instead merely submit that this case ought to make manifest to any but the most jaded conscience the sheer barbarity being done in the name of the Constitution in a country dedicated—at its founding, at least—to the self-evident truth that all human beings "are endowed by their Creator" with an unalienable right to life.

A Failure to Resolve the Issue

Despite the fact that the abortion issue was being worked out state-by-state, the Supreme Court purported to resolve the abortion issue, once and for all and on a nationwide basis, in its 1973 decision in *Roe*. Instead, as Justice Scalia has correctly observed, the Court "fanned into life an issue that has inflamed our national politics" ever since. In 1992, the five-Justice majority in *Casey* "call[ed] the contending sides [on abortion] to end their national division by accepting" what it implausibly claimed was "a common mandate rooted in the Constitution." Thirteen years later, the abortion issue remains as contentious and divisive as ever.

As Justice Scalia suggested in his dissent in *Casey*, Chief Justice Taney surely believed that his *Dred Scott* opinion would resolve, once and for all, the slavery question. But, Scalia continued:

> It is no more realistic for us in this case, than it was for him in that, to think that an issue of the sort they both involved—an issue involving life and death, freedom and subjugation—can be "speedily and finally settled" by the Supreme Court, as President James Buchanan in his inaugural address said the issue of slavery in the territories would be. . . . Quite to the contrary, by foreclosing all democratic outlet for the deep passions this issue arouses, by banishing the issue from the political forum that gives all participants, even the losers, the satisfaction of a fair hearing and an honest fight, by continuing the imposition of a rigid national rule instead of allowing for regional differences, the Court merely prolongs and intensifies the anguish.

> We should get out of this area, where we have no right to be, and where we do neither ourselves nor the country any good by remaining.

As increasing numbers of observers across the political spectrum are coming to recognize, Justice Scalia's prescription in *Casey* remains entirely sound, both as a matter of constitutional law and of judicial statesmanship. If the American people are going to be permitted to exercise their authority as citizens, then all Americans, whatever their views on abortion, should recognize that the Supreme Court's unconstitutional power grab on this issue must end and that the political issue of whether and how to regulate abortions should be returned where it belongs—to the people and to the political processes in the states.

| "In a very real sense, Roe is already history and has been for a long time."

Roe Has Become Irrelevant for Millions of American Women

Laura Kaminker

In the following viewpoint Laura Kaminker predicts that the right to abortion first established in Roe v. Wade *may soon be reversed as more conservative justices are placed on the Supreme Court. But she argues that for millions of women, the right to choose abortion as established in* Roe *has become irrelevant. Congress and the states have passed laws barring public funding of abortions, limiting poor women's access to the procedure. In addition, states have established various restrictions on abortion, including parental consent for minors, waiting periods, and mandatory counseling. Furthermore, many states and localities lack any doctors willing to provide abortions. These developments have had the effect of depriving many women of their reproductive right to choose, she concludes. Kaminker is a freelance writer and activist who volunteers to help women forced to travel to New York City for second-trimester abortions.*

Thirty-two years ago [on January 22, 1973], American women gained greater control over their bodies—and therefore, over their lives—when *Roe v. Wade,* the Supreme Court decision legalizing abortion, became the law of the land.

The choice community celebrates the *Roe* anniversary as a kind of emancipation day, but it is unlikely we will see too many more of those celebrations. *Roe* will almost certainly be reversed soon. Abortion will be legal in some states and not others. State laws will vary widely in the circumstances under which a pregnancy may be terminated—as is now the case, only more so.

However, those of us involved in abortion access know that for millions of American women, *Roe* is already irrelevant.

Financial Obstacles

Money. For a few years after the *Roe* decision, Medicaid paid for abortions; anyone could get an abortion regardless of her age or ability to pay. Only four years later, Congress passed the Hyde Amendment, which banned payment [by Medicaid] for abortions unless the woman's life was endangered. (In 1993, after much struggle, those exceptions were broadened to include cases of rape and incest.)

In most states, Medicaid rarely covers abortion. Yet the cost of a first-trimester abortion can be more than a family on public assistance receives in a month. In our Wal-Mart economy, many working women can't afford a procedure.

Low-income women and girls delay termination as they try to scrape together the money they need. These delays often force them to have second-trimester procedures, which are more complicated medically, more risky—and much more expensive. It is not uncommon for women to carry an unwanted pregnancy to term because they cannot afford a simple medical procedure.

Legal Obstacles

Laws. Then there are the legal obstacles. With the *Webster* (1989) and *Casey* (1992) decisions, the Supreme Court upheld states' rights to restrict access to abortion in myriad ways. Women must jump through hoops and over hurdles before they can terminate a pregnancy. These laws run the gamut of idiocy, from 48-hour waiting periods, to parental consent and notification for minors, to mandatory "counseling," which often involves coercion.

These laws assume women are incompetent, irresponsible, and unable to make their own decisions. They also expose the anti-choice "abortion is murder" argument for the smokescreen that it is. If abortion was murder, these types of laws would be anathema to the anti-choice crowd: what good is delaying murder? However, if one's goal is to control women and punish them for having sex and getting pregnant, then these laws make perfect sense.

But wait, there's more.

Lack of Abortion Providers

Availability. In addition to the financial and legal obstacles, there is one last, often insurmountable obstacle: availability.

Because of anti-choice terrorism and political action, thousands of doctors have stopped providing abortions and thousands of towns have stopped leasing space to abortion providers. Right now, nearly 80% of American women live in a county with no abortion provider. Obtaining an abortion often means traveling long distances, which in turn means finding child care and transportation, and even more funds. Imagine if the state also has a mandatory waiting period, so the entire trip has to be made twice. A baby should not be born because a woman could not afford the price of a bus ticket or had no one to watch her children.

When *Roe* is overturned, I will mourn. But in a very real sense, *Roe* is already history and has been for a long time. Without access, legal abortion is meaningless.

CHAPTER 4

Disputing the Fate of Frozen Embryos

Case Overview

A.Z. v. B.Z. (2000)

Advances in medical technology have given new options to infertile couples and other people who wish to have children. However, they have also raised thorny ethical issues that have, in some instances, been addressed by the courts. The 2000 case of *A.Z. v. B.Z.* is one example of a dispute involving frozen embryos, which are often a by-product of modern fertility treatments.

The Massachusetts case involved a married couple who sought help from a fertility clinic from 1988 through 1991. The woman underwent several treatments in which her eggs were harvested from her ovaries and fertilized with her husband's sperm. Some eggs were implanted in her uterus, while others were frozen and stored for later use. The net result by 1992 was the successful birth of twin daughters—and two vials of leftover embryos.

The clinic required its patients to sign consent forms stating what they wanted done with these embryos. Both the husband and wife signed forms stating that, in the event they became separated, the embryos would be given to the wife for implantation. In 1995, the wife, without the husband's knowledge, tried to have more children using some of the embryos. The attempt failed, and the husband filed for divorce. He sought a permanent injunction forbidding his estranged wife from "using" the remaining frozen embryos.

A probate judge found in favor of the husband, ruling that his right to avoid procreation outweighed the woman's right to use the embryos to try to have additional children. The case was ultimately appealed and heard by the Massachusetts Supreme Judicial Court. That court ruled that, previous written agreements notwithstanding, the government should not compel a person to become a parent against his or her will.

This decision attracted criticism from those who believed that the wife's reproductive rights were violated and that the husband had already made a legal commitment to parenthood by participating in the fertility treatment procedures and signing the requisite consent forms. In addition, some pro-life activists criticized the decision on the grounds that such cases should not only consider the respective rights of the two spouses, but also the rights of the frozen embryos themselves.

A.Z. v. B.Z. is one of several cases in which state judges have acted as legal arbiters in disputes over whose reproductive rights should prevail. Some people have argued that these cases raise public policy issues that should be resolved at the national level. Thus the fate of frozen embryos may one day be decided by Congressional legislation or a Supreme Court ruling.

| "As a matter of public policy, we conclude that forced procreation is not an area amenable to judicial enforcement."

The Court's Decision: Society Should Not Force People to Become Parents

Judith A. Cowin

Judith A. Cowin is a justice of the Massachusetts Supreme Judicial Court. On March 31, 2000, writing for a unanimous seven-member court, she issued a ruling that upheld a lower court's decision in A.Z. v. B.Z., a case involving a divorced couple's dispute over what to do with frozen embryos (Cowin uses the term preembryos) left over from earlier infertility treatments. The wife (B.Z.) wanted to implant the embryos and attempt to have more children. Although the husband (A.Z.) had signed a consent form agreeing to allow the wife to do just that if the couple separated, a family court ruled—and Cowin and her associates agreed—that the husband should not be forced to become a father against his wishes. The following excerpts from Cowin's ruling include a brief family history of the dispute, the reasons why the court believes the husband's consent form should not be considered binding, and a determination that the law cannot be used to compel people to enter family relationships (such as parenthood) against their wishes.

We transferred this case to this court on our own motion to consider for the first time the effect of a consent form between a married couple and an in vitro fertilization (IVF) clinic (clinic) concerning disposition of frozen preembryos. B.Z., the former wife (wife) of A.Z. (husband), appeals

Judith A. Cowin, ruling, *A.Z. v. B.Z.,* SJC 08098, March 31, 2000.

from a judgment of the Probate and Family Court that included a permanent injunction in favor of the husband, prohibiting the wife "from utilizing" the frozen preembryos held in cryopreservation at the clinic. . . . On February 8, 2000, we issued an order affirming the judgment of the Probate and Family Court. . . . This opinion states the reasons for that order.

Attempts to Have Children

1. Factual background. We recite the relevant background facts as determined by the probate judge in his detailed findings of fact after a hearing concerning disposition of the preembryos at which both the husband and wife were separately represented by counsel. The probate judge's findings are supplemented by the record where necessary.

a. History of the couple. The husband and wife were married in 1977. For the first two years of their marriage they resided in Virginia, where they both served in the armed forces. While in Virginia, they encountered their first difficulties conceiving a child and underwent fertility testing. During their stay in Virginia the wife did become pregnant, but she suffered an ectopic pregnancy [where the fertilized egg implants in the fallopian tube instead of the uterus], as a result of which she miscarried and her left fallopian tube was removed.

In 1980, the husband and wife moved to Maryland where they underwent additional fertility treatment. The treatment lasted one year and did not result in a pregnancy. In 1988, the wife was transferred to Massachusetts and the husband remained in Maryland to continue his schooling. After arriving in Massachusetts, the wife began IVF treatments at an IVF clinic here. . . .

IVF involves injecting the woman with fertility drugs in order to stimulate production of eggs which can be surgically retrieved or harvested. After the eggs are removed, they are combined in a petri dish with sperm produced by the man, on the same day as the egg removal, in an effort to fertilize the eggs. If fertilization between any of the eggs and sperm occurs, preembryos are formed that are held in a petri dish for one or two days until a decision can be made as to which preembryos will be used immediately and which will be frozen and stored by the clinic for later use. Preembryos that are to be utilized immediately are not frozen. . . .

As a result of the 1991 treatment, the wife conceived and gave birth to twin daughters in 1992. During the 1991 IVF treatment, more preembryos were formed than were necessary for immediate implantation, and two vials of preembryos were frozen for possible future implantation.

In the spring of 1995, before the couple separated, the wife desired more children and had one of the remaining vials of preembryos thawed and one preembryo was implanted. She did so without informing her husband. The husband learned of this when he received a notice from his insurance company regarding the procedure. During this period relations between the husband and wife deteriorated. The wife sought and received a protective order against the husband A. Ultimately, they separated and the husband filed for divorce.

At the time of the divorce, one vial containing four frozen preembryos remained in storage at the clinic. Using one or more of these preembryos, it is possible that the wife could conceive; the likelihood of conception depends, inter alia, on the condition of the preembryos which cannot be ascertained until the preembryos are thawed. The husband filed a motion to obtain a permanent injunction, prohibiting the wife from "using" the remaining vial of frozen preembryos.

Consent Forms

b. The IVF clinic and the consent forms. In order to participate in fertility treatment, . . . the clinic required egg and sperm donors (donors) to sign certain consent forms for the relevant procedures. Each time before removal of the eggs from the wife, the clinic required the husband and wife in this case to sign a preprinted consent form concerning ultimate disposition of the frozen preembryos. The wife signed a number of forms on which the husband's signature was not required. The only forms that both the husband and the wife were required to sign were those entitled "Consent Form for Freezing (Cryopreservation) of Embryos" (consent form), one of which is the form at issue here.

Each consent form explains the general nature of the IVF procedure and outlines the freezing process, including the financial cost and the potential benefits and risks of that process. The consent form also requires the donors to decide the disposition of the frozen preembryos on certain listed contingencies: "wife or donor" reaching normal menopause or age forty-five years; preembryos no longer being healthy; "one of us dying;" "[s]hould we become separated"; "[s]hould we both die." Under each contingency the consent form provides the following as options for disposition of the preembryos: "donated or destroyed—choose one or both." A blank line beneath these choices permits the donors to write in additional alternatives not listed as options on the form, and the form notifies the donors that they may do so. The consent form also informs the donors that they may change their minds as to any disposition, provided that both donors convey that fact in writing to the clinic. . . .

c. The execution of the forms. Every time before eggs were retrieved from the wife and combined with sperm from the husband, they each signed a consent form. The husband was present when the first form was completed by the wife in October, 1988. They both signed that consent form after it was finished. The form, as filled out by the wife, stated, inter alia, that if they "[s]hould become separated, [they] both

141

agree[d] to have the embryo(s) ... return[ed] to [the] wife for implant." The husband and wife thereafter underwent six additional egg retrievals for freezing and signed six additional consent forms, one each in June, 1989, and February, 1989, two forms in December, 1989, and one each in August, 1990, and August, 1991. The August, 1991, consent form governs the vial of frozen preembryos now stored at the clinic. ...

Past Legal Decisions

2. The Probate Court's decision. The probate judge concluded that, while donors are generally free to agree as to the ultimate disposition of frozen preembryos, the agreement at issue was unenforceable because of "change in circumstances" occurring during the four years after the husband and wife signed the last, and governing, consent form in 1991: the birth of the twins as a result of the IVF procedure, the wife's obtaining a protective order against the husband, the husband's filing for a divorce, and the wife's then seeking "to thaw the preembryos for implantation in the hopes of having additional children." The probate judge concluded that "[n]o agreement should be enforced in equity when intervening events have changed the circumstances such that the agreement which was originally signed did not contemplate the actual situation now facing the parties." In the absence of a binding agreement, the judge determined that the "best solution" was to balance the wife's interest in procreation against the husband's interest in avoiding procreation. Based on his findings, the judge determined that the husband's interest in avoiding procreation outweighed the wife's interest in having additional children and granted the permanent injunction in favor of the husband.

3. Legal background. While IVF has been available for over two decades and has been the focus of much academic commentary, there is little law on the enforceability of agreements concerning the disposition of frozen preembryos. Only three

States have enacted legislation addressing the issue.

Two State courts of last resort, the Supreme Court of Tennessee and the Court of Appeals of New York, have dealt with the enforceability of agreements between donors regarding the disposition of preembryos and have concluded that such agreements should ordinarily be enforced. . . .

Why the Consent Form Should Not Be Enforced

4. Legal analysis. This is the first reported case involving the disposition of frozen preembryos in which a consent form signed between the donors on the one hand and the clinic on the other provided that, on the donors' separation, the preembryos were to be given to one of the donors for implantation. In view of the purpose of the form (drafted by and to give assistance to the clinic) and the circumstances of execution, we are dubious at best that it represents the intent of the husband and the wife regarding disposition of the preembryos in the case of a dispute between them. In any event, for several independent reasons, we conclude that the form should not be enforced in the circumstances of this case.

First, the consent form's primary purpose is to explain to the donors the benefits and risks of freezing, and to record the donors' desires for disposition of the frozen preembryos at the time the form is executed in order to provide the clinic with guidance if the donors (as a unit) no longer wish to use the frozen preembryos. The form does not state, and the record does not indicate, that the husband and wife intended the consent form to act as a binding agreement between them should they later disagree as to the disposition. Rather, it appears that it was intended only to define the donors' relationship as a unit with the clinic.

Second, the consent form does not contain a duration provision. The wife sought to enforce this particular form four years after it was signed by the husband in significantly

143

changed circumstances and over the husband's objection. In the absence of any evidence that the donors agreed on the time period during which the consent form was to govern their conduct, we cannot assume that the donors intended the consent form to govern the disposition of the frozen preembryos four years after it was executed, especially in light of the fundamental change in their relationship (i.e., divorce).

Third, the form uses the term "[s]hould we become separated" in referring to the disposition of the frozen preembryos without defining "become separated." Because this dispute arose in the context of a divorce, we cannot conclude that the consent form was intended to govern in these circumstances. Separation and divorce have distinct legal meanings. Legal changes occur by operation of law when a couple divorces that do not occur when a couple separates. Because divorce legally ends a couple's marriage, we shall not assume, in the absence of any evidence to the contrary, that an agreement on this issue providing for separation was meant to govern in the event of a divorce. . . .

Finally, the consent form is not a separation agreement that is binding on the couple in a divorce proceeding. . . . The consent form does not contain provisions for custody, support, and maintenance, in the event that the wife conceives and gives birth to a child. . . . In summary, the consent form is legally insufficient in several important respects and does not approach the minimum level of completeness needed to denominate it as an enforceable contract in a dispute between the husband and the wife.

A Matter of Public Policy

With this said, we conclude that, even had the husband and the wife entered into an unambiguous agreement between themselves regarding the disposition of the frozen preembryos, we would not enforce an agreement that would compel one donor to become a parent against his or her will. As a matter of public policy, we conclude that forced procreation is not an area amenable to judicial enforcement. It is well-established that courts will not enforce contracts that violate public policy. . . .

The [Massachusetts] Legislature has already determined by statute that individuals should not be bound by certain agreements binding them to enter or not enter into familial relationships. . . .

Similarly, this court has expressed its hesitancy to become involved in intimate questions inherent in the marriage relationship. . . .

In our decisions, we have also indicated a reluctance to enforce prior agreements that bind individuals to future family relationships. . . . We held that a surrogacy agreement in which the surrogate mother agreed to give up the child on its birth is unenforceable unless the agreement contained, inter alia, a "reasonable" waiting period during which the mother could change her mind. . . . We determined, as an expression of public policy, that a contract requiring an individual to abandon a marriage is unenforceable. And, in the same spirit, we stated . . . that agreements providing for a general restraint against marriage are unenforceable.

We glean from these statutes and judicial decisions that prior agreements to enter into familial relationships (marriage or parenthood) should not be enforced against individuals who subsequently reconsider their decisions. . . .

We derive from existing State laws and judicial precedent a public policy in this Commonwealth that individuals shall not be compelled to enter into intimate family relationships, and that the law shall not be used as a mechanism for forcing such relationships when they are not desired. This policy is grounded in the notion that respect for liberty and privacy requires that individuals be accorded the freedom to decide whether to enter into a family relationship. . . .

In this case, we are asked to decide whether the law of the Commonwealth [of Massachusetts] may compel an individual to become a parent over his or her contemporaneous objection. The husband signed this consent form in 1991. Enforcing the form against him would require him to become a parent over his present objection to such an undertaking. We decline to do so.

"As a precedent from an influential state court, the decision [in A.Z. v. B.Z.] places an even greater wedge between biological reality and legal dictate."

A.Z. v. B.Z. Denies the Rights of Embryos

Daniel Avila

Daniel Avila is associate director of public policy for the Massachusetts Catholic Conference, the office that advocates the official positions of the Roman Catholic Church with respect to policy issues in Massachusetts. In the following selection he criticizes the decision of the Massachusetts Supreme Judicial Court in the case of A.Z. v. B.Z., in which a divorced woman was prevented from implanting embryos created in fertility treatments received during her marriage because of objections from her former husband. Avila argues that the justices in the Massachusetts court erred in saying that a prior consent agreement by the husband was unenforceable and amounted to "forced procreation." In addition to signing an advance form, Avila maintains, the husband had agreed to procreation when he contributed sperm to help make the embryos. Avila further contends that the embryos themselves should be given greater legal standing than the Massachusetts court afforded them. By asserting that the embryos were in fact "preembryos," the court left them with no legal parents and no legal rights.

Last month [March 2000], the Massachusetts Supreme Judicial Court (SJC) issued an opinion that added an entirely different and ominous meaning to the statement that "life begins at conception". Traditional understandings of procreation and parenthood also took a hit in a ruling that appears to open the door to the wholesale destruction of frozen embryos in Massachusetts.

The case of *A.Z. v. B.Z.* turned on the question of what happens to frozen embryos when the mother wants them implanted and the father does not. The four embryos at stake in the case were created consensually in 1991 by *in vitro* fertilization before the couple was divorced in 1995. The dispute over the embryos arose when the father, in the course of the divorce proceeding, learned of the mother's desire to implant them and filed for an injunction preventing her from doing so against his wishes.

The Trial Judge's Decision

In 1996, a Massachusetts trial judge found for the father, citing the Tennessee *Davis v. Davis* decision in 1990 permitting the destruction of frozen embryos when the parents could not agree to their disposition. Noting that the embryos were frozen at the four-cell stage, the judge ruled that they did not possess the legal status of personhood in Massachusetts and thus were not protected by state custody laws. Despite the fact that the couple had signed consent forms directing that the embryos be implanted even should the parents separate, the judge found that the forms were not binding because of the divorce.

The judge held that absent an enforceable contract the constitutional rights of the couple had to be weighed, and concluded that the father's rights prevailed over the mother's rights because he would face "emotional burdens" from "unwanted parenthood" if the embryos were implanted. The judge also argued that implantation would be "unfair to a child who would enter the world unwanted by one of his or her parents."

The mother's attorney appealed solely on the contract issue, and did not challenge the lower court's personhood ruling. The father left the state and did not bother to contest the appeal. The SJC decided to hear the case directly, but delayed a hearing until 1999 because the lower court had lost certain records that needed to be reproduced. This lent urgency to the deliberations because the fertility clinic had advised the mother that any attempt to bring the embryos to term would be medically futile because of the mother's age after June 2000.

In February of this year [2000], the SJC issued a brief order in the father's favor, promising to release a full opinion later. On March 31, Justice Judith A. Cowin, writing for the unanimous seven-member court, agreed with the trial judge that the consent forms were not binding on the father.

Forced Procreation?

Yet she rejected the use of a balancing test that might have given mothers in some cases at least a theoretical chance to override a father's objection to the implantation of their embryos. She found instead that implantation in any case where the couple is split over what to do with the embryos would "compel one donor to become a parent against his or her will", and that "forced procreation" was against public policy! Thus, frozen embryos could never be implanted when the father refuses consent, even if the mother proved the father had earlier made an otherwise enforceable agreement to consent.

Because the decision relied on an interpretation of Massachusetts public policy, the mother appears to have no recourse for appealing to the U.S. Supreme Court, and time is running out anyway for her to successfully bear the embryos, thus effectively rendering any appeal moot. News reports are mixed about whether the embryos will be thawed and left to die or destroyed outright.

What did Justice Cowin mean by concluding as a matter of law that implanting the already existing embryos would be "forced procreation"? Webster's Dictionary defines procreation as "the act of begetting; generation and production of young". To beget, Webster's indicates, is "to cause to exist."

As pointed out by a friend of the court brief filed by the Catholic Medical Association and other groups, "the 'procreation' involving the father's bodily donation of sperm has already occurred with the father's consent, resulting in the conception of the embryos." The reality of the embryos' creation and existence will not change by some mysterious biological process if the father succeeds in preventing their implantation in his ex-wife's womb. As the brief put it, "The embryos rest in frozen storage, real, not imaginary products of the father's consensual participation in their beginning.". . .

One finds the key to Justice Cowin's remarkable legal conclusion in her discussion of the case's facts. She informed the reader on the opinion's first page that the court will refer to the embryos as "preembryos", and cited without any further explanation a 1994 report of the American Fertility Society. The Report has attracted substantial scientific criticism. Contrary to the consensus among embryologists, the Report coins the term preembryos in an effort to demonstrate that human beings do not begin to exist at fertilization.

When Life Begins

Justice Cowin then sidestepped the debate over when life begins by asserting matter of factly and without argument that the embryos are not yet "conceived" or "procreated" and would not be unless and until they are implanted with the consent of both parents. As a consequence, the father is not yet to be considered a parent responsible for the survival of his children and the mother is not yet a parent with the right to custody of her children. Parenthood is, the opinion suggests, entirely a matter of where the children are physically located and of who wants to be in a social relationship with them rather than a consequence of biology.

And if the "donors" were in agreement rather than at odds, Justice Cowin's opinion appears to free them to do whatever they please with their frozen embryos, including selling the embryos for research or destroying them, because they are not subject to the obligations of legal parenthood. The law would not require their implantation. This means that all of the frozen embryos in the Commonwealth [or Massachusetts] have, in effect, no legal parents, and now certainly have no legal rights.

Impact of the Decision

While the *A.Z. v. B.Z.* decision raises numerous problems in Massachusetts, it will undoubtedly have an impact outside of Massachusetts as well. As a precedent from an influential state court, the decision places an even greater wedge between biological reality and legal dictate. It ratifies (although it does not mention it) the controversial policy adopted a few years ago by the American College of Obstetricians and Gynecologists that redefines the moment of conception as occurring at implantation and not at fertilization. And it forces pro-lifers to reconsider any educational campaign that asserts, without further explanation, that life begins at conception.

The most disturbing aspect of the opinion is the value that it assigns to the children involved, that is, none at all in the law's eyes. The decision is yet another unfortunate sign that "family" has become merely a construct of desire regardless of biology and no longer serves as a haven for the nurturing of children.

| "As the use of in-vitro fertilization grows,
so does the conundrum of what to do
with unused frozen embryos."

Ethical Dilemmas Raised by Unused Embryos

Jane Eisner

Jane Eisner is a columnist for the Philadelphia Inquirer. *The following selection, taken from a 2001 article, focuses on a New Jersey frozen-embryo dispute that has several similarities to the Massachusetts case of A.Z. v. B.Z. In both instances, a divorced couple disagreed over what should be done with embryos created during infertility treatment and placed in frozen storage. In the New Jersey case, a court ultimately ruled in favor of the wife and her wish to have the embryos destroyed. After examining the circumstances of the New Jersey dispute, Eisner goes on to argue that society and the legal system have not kept up with advances in medical technology, raising many unanswered questions about the right to procreate, the right not to procreate, and the legal and moral status of frozen embryos. The failure of governments to enact appropriate laws has added to the confusion, she maintains, as has the varying rulings of state courts in frozen-embryo cases.*

The case of the frozen embryos, argued last week [in February 2001] in New Jersey, is a classic example of what happens when sophisticated reproductive technology collides with the age-old passion to reproduce and the fragility of modern relationships.

Here's a couple who went through great trouble and expense to become pregnant through in-vitro fertilization, only to divorce a few years later. Held hostage by this marital breakup are not the car or the silverware, but seven frozen embryos that the mother wants to discard and the father wants to keep for some future purpose.

Since the couple had no written agreement detailing how to dispose of unused embryos, it will be up to the justices of the state Supreme Court to decide whether these microscopic zygotes are to remain in arctic limbo or thawed and then shrivel away.

This is what we have in America today: 21st century medicine governed by 19th century law. As the only advanced country without a national policy on reproductive technology, we are left with a hodgepodge of conflicting state laws—or more commonly, no laws at all.

As Art Caplan, head of the University of Pennsylvania's Center for Bioethics puts it: "We're operating a space shuttle with the moral navigation system of [Christopher Columbus's ship,] the *Santa Maria*."

Ethical Dilemmas

The issues raised by a case like the one in New Jersey exemplify the current reproductive quandary. Are embryos considered property, or a sort of pre-human being, or the beginning of life itself—even though fertilized sperm and eggs must travel through many biological hoops before becoming a fetus?

Is there a right to procreate? Is there a right not to procreate? Does a woman, who carries and then delivers a baby, have more right to decide than a man? How do we even define parenthood in this brave new world?

These ethical dilemmas, complex though they are, are not the only obstacles keeping the country from developing humane and useful reproductive policies. This is as much a political problem as a philosophical one. Well-meaning efforts to provide minimum regulation have been stymied by strong opposition and a lack of political will.

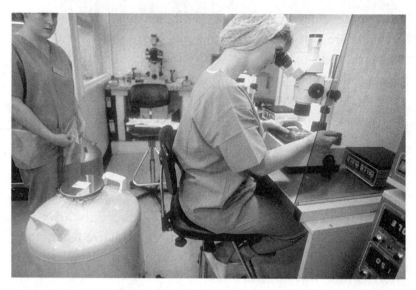

A technician examines frozen embryos at a fertility clinic. The fate of unused frozen embryos has opened up worldwide debate on their legal and moral status. © Matthew Polak/ CORBIS SYGMA

As the use of in-vitro fertilization grows, so does the conundrum of what to do with unused frozen embryos. There are at least 80,000 embryos now frozen in labs and clinics in this country—some say the true count is double that number—and up to 20,000 may be the subject of dispute.

Many of these disputes could be resolved without court intervention if only the couple had been forced to spell out their wishes, in detail, before the first egg and sperm were placed in a petri dish.

Some IVF clinics require this type of directive; others do not. The industry is like the Wild, Wild West, gung-ho and resistant to regulation. And, of course, couples considering IVF treatment probably don't ever imagine that their embryos might outlive their marriage.

Yet, that's just what happened in New Jersey, where J.B. (the ex-wife) and M.B. (the ex-husband) are fighting over an oral agreement in which he said she promised that the embryos would not be destroyed.

Advance Directives Might Help

This dispute might have been averted had legislation introduced by New Jersey Assemblyman Neil Cohen, D., Union, been law before the Bs' embryos were first stored in a Marlton [New Jersey] lab. Cohen's bill requires that couples complete written directives in advance on what should happen to the embryos they create.

It's the reproductive version of a living will—forcing the parties to think through scenarios and express legally binding intent. While not a panacea, it could go a long way toward rationalizing this chaotic corner of reproductive law.

What if the couple divorces? What if one of them dies or becomes mentally incapacitated? What if they simply fail to pay the storage fees?

This bill makes too much sense to be bottled up in committee for more than a year, but that's the story in Trenton. Even worse has been the response to a similar bill introduced in New York by State Sen. Roy Goodman, a Manhattan Republican. It's been in limbo since 1998.

Court Confusion

Without the guidance of lawmakers, individual courts have been left to decide these cases, and that has prompted even more confusion. New Jersey's is the fourth state Supreme Court to take a frozen embryos case; each circumstance is different, yes, but so are the values expressed in each opinion.

New York's judges ruled that a contract is a contract. The Massachusetts court agreed—except if one partner wanted out, as the husband did in that case. "We would not enforce an agreement that would compel one donor to become a parent against his or her will," the court ruled in *A.Z. v. B.Z.*

Tennessee's court ruled that the embryos are entitled to "special respect." That ruling was in 1992, and experts are still trying to figure out what that phrase means.

Other countries are further along. In Great Britain, frozen embryos can be kept no longer than five years unless a couple directs otherwise. French law also applies the five-year limit. But in the United States, even the American Bar Association hasn't agreed on a model act that addresses reproductive technology.

Legislation alone won't smooth the rocky terrain of this uncertain new world. A contract may be a contract—but should a sperm or egg donor always be a parent? Is it morally defensible to force someone to be a biological father or mother against his or her will?

It's the silence on these issues that is most damaging. In the absence of national debate and policy, couples, clinics and courts are rogue actors in what should be a communal play. The stakes couldn't be higher, and yet, as Art Caplan so wryly notes, the fate of embryos preserved at minus-196 degrees Celsius "is in the hands of PECO [an energy utility]."

Let's hope the power stays on in Marlton until we figure this out.

"To date, public policy has favored gamete donors who, despite their prior consent, wish to avoid procreation with their
former spouse."

Embryo Disputes Have Led to Reduced Reproductive Rights

Judith F. Daar

*Judith F. Daar is a law professor at Whittier College in Costa
Mesa, California. In the following viewpoint she examines four
state court cases, including A.Z. v. B.Z., that involved divorced
couples battling over the disposition of frozen embryos. She concludes that while the state courts used various legal analyses and
reasoning, all ultimately sided with the person who wanted to
avoid procreation. She contends that the direction state courts
are taking signifies a potential step back for privacy and reproductive rights.*

In recent years, courts have increasingly found themselves
arbiters of disputes in the emotionally charged area of assisted reproductive technologies. Legal disputes are hardly surprising in the world of infertility medicine, where millions of
patients spend billions of dollars in efforts to have a child. Increasingly, these efforts produce embryos that are frozen for
later use, at once maximizing a couple's chances for success
and minimizing the medical intrusiveness that necessarily ac-
companies most forms of assisted reproductive technologies.
But with over 100,000 embryos in frozen storage in the United

Judith F. Daar, "Frozen Embryo Disputes Revisited: A Trilogy of Procreation Avoidance
Approaches," *Journal of Law, Medicine & Ethics,* vol. 29, Summer 2001, p. 197. Copyright © 2001 by the American Society of Law & Medicine, Inc. Reproduced by permission.

States and a divorce rate of 40 to 50 percent, it is not surprising that disputes over the disposition of these embryos are arising, causing the legal landscape surrounding these technologies to continue to expand.

The most recent addition to the jurisprudence is *A.Z. v. B.Z.*, a case decided by the Massachusetts Supreme Judicial Court on March 31, 2000. . . .

The Massachusetts Supreme Judicial Court is the third of three state high courts to issue a written decision involving a frozen embryo dispute. Interestingly, each of these three courts has reached the same factual result, but for very different reasons. In each case, the court favored the party wishing to avoid procreation. To make sense of the jurisprudence of embryo dispositions, one needs to look at how each court has approached the parties' claims for ultimate control over the embryos they produced with their estranged spouses. In addition to analyzing these three opinions, I will also discuss a fourth case, *J.B. v. M.B.*, decided by the New Jersey Superior Court according to the reasoning used in *A.Z. v. B.Z.*

Davis v. Davis: Enforceability of Any Prior Agreement

The first high court to consider the embryo disposition dilemma was the Tennessee Supreme Court, whose 1992 decision in *Davis v. Davis* has become the starting point for each successive court's analysis. In *Davis,* the court set out a three-part test to be applied when a couple disagrees over the disposition of their cryopreserved embryos. Briefly stated, the *Davis* test looks first to the preferences of the progenitors. Next, if the gamete donors disagree over disposition, or if their preferences cannot be ascertained, courts are directed to enforce any prior agreements between the parties. The *Davis* court contemplated that such agreements might include an informed consent document signed by the couple at the behest of their treating infertility clinic, but other agreements between the parties were not ruled out. Finally, in the absence of a prior agreement, courts are advised to balance the relative interests of the parties. When those interests are in equipoise, courts are advised to favor the party wishing to avoid procreation, as long as the other party "has a reasonable possibility of achieving parenthood by means other than use of the preembryos in question." This third prong of procreation avoidance was applied to the couple in *Davis* because they had not previously expressed their preferences in any formal writing.

Kass v. Kass: Presumed Enforceability

In *Kass v. Kass*, the New York Court of Appeals became the second state high court to rule in an embryo dispute matter. In this case, the court agreed with the *Davis* court that prior agreements governing embryo disposition should be presumed valid and enforced. The Kasses had signed several documents at the request of their in vitro fertilization provider addressing possible future contingencies. The documents, though inconsistent and ambiguous, were viewed by the New York high court as showing a clear intent that the parties wished to donate their cryopreserved embryos to research in the event of divorce. Thus, procreation avoidance prevailed again, albeit under the guise of contract adherence.

A.Z. v. B.Z.: No Enforceability

When the Massachusetts Supreme Judicial Court agreed, on its own motion, to consider the enforceability of embryo disposition agreements, court observers wondered whether the *Davis-Kass* "presumed enforceability" principle could withstand the cold hard facts in *A.Z. v. B.Z.* After all, the Massachusetts couple signed seven separate agreements calling for placement with the wife who was seeking to elect, rather than avoid, procreation. Perhaps in a tribute to the adage "hard facts make bad law," the court, without adopting or rejecting the "presumed enforceability" test, instead ruled that the specific agreement in this case should not be enforced. . . . The court set out numerous objections to enforceability, including imprecise language, changed circumstances, ambiguous wording, and flawed intent, but it ultimately relied on the public policy rationale of procreation avoidance.

It remains unclear whether all Massachusetts preconception agreements are unenforceable, or only those that might compel one party to become a parent against his or her wishes, however subsequently expressed. In *A.Z.*, the court noted in a footnote that while forced procreation is unacceptable, enforceability of an agreement calling for destruction or donation of embryos for research is still an open question. This footnote provides a hint that the court has not entirely rejected the *Davis-Kass* contract principles. Thus, presumed enforceability of prior agreements remains an option, as long as the agreement adheres to the public policy sensibilities of the state's highest court. While courts clearly have the discretion to decide cases on public policy grounds, the public policy rationale set forth in *A.Z.* is troubling because it is based on the false notion that forced parenthood is never a judicially sanctioned outcome.

J.B. v. M.B.: Following Massachusetts's Lead

The reasoning employed in *A.Z*, has already proven influential with another court. On June 1, 2000, the Appellate Division of the New Jersey Superior Court issued its decision in *J.B. v. M.B.*, a case involving the now familiar scenario of a divorcing couple disputing the disposition of their frozen embryos. In a case of gender role reversal, however, the husband in *J.B.* sought control of the embryos to use with a future wife or for donation to an infertile couple, while his ex-wife wanted the embryos destroyed. The relevant preconception agreements in this case consisted of an alleged oral agreement in which the husband and wife consented to donate any unused embryos and a written agreement providing for relinquishment of "our tissues" in the event of divorce to the in vitro fertilization clinic. This formal agreement seemed to play no role in the decision, as the court focused instead on the wife's alleged agreement to allow another couple to use the remaining embryos.

After reviewing the decisions in *Davis* and *Kass*, the New Jersey court lauded the decision in *A.Z.* for its focus on public policy concerns. The court referenced and thereafter adopted the pronouncement of the Massachusetts high court that "agreements to enter into familial relationships (marriage or parenthood) should not be enforced against individuals who subsequently reconsider their decisions." The court reasoned, moreover, that a decision favoring the wife does not impair the husband's right to procreate, as he retains the capacity to father children. But allowing the wife's biological child to be born and potentially raised by strangers was deemed "understandably unacceptable to the wife."

The case for procreation avoidance is far stronger under the facts in *J.B.* than in the three previous high court decisions in which the ex-wife was denied use of disputed frozen embryos. Allowing a woman to control the fate of preimplantation embryos is consistent with the jurisprudence of abortion, which gives women (versus men) the exclusive right to decide whether to terminate or continue an early pregnancy. Deciding whether to implant or discard frozen embryos can be likened to a decision about the desirability of an early pregnancy, a decision vested only in the female. Thus, the increasingly popular procreation avoidance standard adds a new dimension to our understanding of reproductive liberties. Currently, when an early embryo is extracorporeal rather than *in vivo*, a woman's exclusive control of that embryo must yield to her male partner's desire to avoid procreation. While courts view this shift in the balance of power as the only way to uphold a public policy against forced parenthood, it must also be recognized as disparate treatment of fertile and infertile women. On balance, it appears that in the world of assisted reproductive technologies, the perceived harm of forced parenthood outweighs any harms arising from the deprivation of reproductive rights.

The Future of Preconception Agreements

The cases addressing preconception agreements, though each employs distinct reasoning, seem united in their adoption of procreation avoidance to resolve disputes over frozen embryos. What remains unclear is the effect these judicial decisions will have on couples and individuals who seek the services and counsel of infertility clinics. Can a couple in Tennessee or New York rely on those courts' pledge of presumed enforceability in the face of an unambiguous agreement to award embryos to the party wishing to procreate? If a future Massachusetts court opposes embryo research on public policy grounds, will a couple there be deprived of the opportunity to donate spare embryos for research purposes? What will be the fate of couples in states that have not yet weighed in on this debate? Clearly, no couple can feel entirely secure in the interpretation and enforceability of their written preconception agreements in our current jurisprudential environment.

The truth is that embryo disposition agreements have been both lauded and attacked for the way they shape family decision-making. For some, they represent an opportunity for clear reflection and careful planning, while others view them as an inappropriate usurpation of individual contemporaneous choice. Regardless of the perceived merits of such agreements, it is clear that in the increasingly form-based practice of reproductive medicine, written disclosures will continue to dominate the consent process. Current practices in infertility clinics rely on a single, albeit lengthy, document that includes provisions informing patients of the risks and alternatives of various treatment modalities (the informed-consent portion) as well as how the gametes and embryos will be disposed of under various future scenarios (the disposition portion). It has been suggested that giving patients a single form containing both informed-consent and disposition information is confusing and unlikely to produce informed choices. Instead, informed-consent and disposition documents should be bifurcated and discussed with patients at different times. That way, patients can more fully understand their treatment options before making contingency plans for disposition in the event of death or divorce. . . .

The increased judicial and legislative attention now focused on preconception disposition agreements may be a welcome improvement to the overall quality of infertility care. More than ever, patients are acutely aware that the choices they make at the outset of treatment may profoundly affect its ultimate course. Recent case law suggests, however, that patient control may be an illusion if a reviewing court perceives the patient's choice to be against public policy. To date, public policy has favored gamete donors who, despite their prior consent, wish to avoid procreation with their former spouse. While this might be the public policy most favored by our society, we should recognize that it is achieved at the expense of private decision-making and potentially in derogation of treasured reproductive liberties.

Organizations to Contact

ACLU Reproductive Freedom Project
125 Broad St., 18th Fl., New York, NY 10004-2400
(212) 549-2500 • fax: (212) 549-2652
Web site: www.aclu.org

A branch of the American Civil Liberties Union, the project coordinates efforts in litigation, advocacy, and public education to guarantee the constitutional right to reproductive choice. The project disseminates fact sheets, pamphlets, and editorial articles and publishes the quarterly newsletter *Reproductive Rights Update.*

Alan Guttmacher Institute
120 Wall St., 21st Fl., New York, NY 10005
(212) 248-1111 • fax: (212) 248-1951
e-mail: info@guttmacher.org
Web site: www.agi-usa.org

The institute is a reproduction research group that advocates the right to safe and legal abortion. It provides extensive statistical information on abortion and voluntary population control. Its publications include the bimonthly journal *Family Planning Perspectives.*

American Society for Reproductive Medicine (ASRM)
1209 Montgomery Hwy., Birmingham, AL 35216
(205) 978-5000 • fax: (205) 978-5005
e-mail: asrm@asrm.org
Web site: www.asrm.org

The American Society for Reproductive Medicine (formerly the American Fertility Society) is composed of more than ten thousand physicians and scientists interested in studying fertility in humans and animals and in researching and treating infertility. ASRM also publishes the monthly journal *Fertility and Sterility* and the quarterly newsletter *Fertility News.*

Center for Reproductive Rights
120 Wall St., New York, NY 10005
(917) 637-3600 • fax: (917) 637-3666
e-mail: info@reprorights.org
Web site: www.crlp.org

The center is a nonprofit legal advocacy organization dedicated to promoting and defending women's reproductive rights worldwide. Its Web site offers current legal news and medical information about legal advocacy, human rights, equality, adolescents, safe pregnancies, contraception, and abortion, detailed for individual states and around the world.

Human Life Foundation (HLF)
215 Lexington Ave., New York, NY 10016
(212) 685-5210 • fax: (212) 725-9793
e-mail: humanlifereview@mindspring.com
Web site: www.humanlifereview.com

The foundation serves as a charitable and educational support group for individuals opposed to abortion, euthanasia, and infanticide. It also offers financial support to organizations that provide women with alternatives to abortion. HLF's publications include the quarterly *Human Life Review* and books and pamphlets on abortion, bioethics, and family issues.

National Abortion and Reproductive Rights Action League (NARAL)
1156 Fifteenth St. NW, Suite 700, Washington, DC 20005
(202) 973-3000 • fax: (202) 973-3096
e-mail: comments@naral.org
Web site: www.naral.org

Now known officially as NARAL Pro-Choice America, NARAL works to develop and sustain a pro-choice political constituency in order to maintain the right of all women to legal abortion. The league briefs members of Congress and testifies at hearings on abortion and related issues. It publishes the quarterly *NARAL Newsletter*.

National Right to Life Committee (NRLC)
512 Tenth St. NW, Washington, DC 20004
(202) 626-8800
e-mail: nrlc@nrlc.org
Web site: www.nrlc.org

NRLC is one of the largest organizations opposing abortion. It encourages ratification of a constitutional amendment granting embryos and fetuses the same right to life as postnatal persons. NRLC publishes the brochure *When Does Life Begin?* and the periodic tabloid *National Right to Life News.*

Planned Parenthood Federation of America (PPFA)
810 Seventh Ave., New York, NY 10019
(212) 541-7800 • fax: (212) 245-1845
e-mail: communications@ppfa.org
Web site: www.ppfa.org

PPFA is a national organization that supports people's right to make their own reproductive decisions without governmental interference. It provides contraception, abortion, and family planning services at clinics located throughout the United States. Among its extensive publications are the pamphlets *Abortions: Questions and Answers, Five Ways to Prevent Abortion,* and *Nine Reasons Why Abortions Are Legal.*

For Further Research

Books

Hadley Arkes, *Natural Rights and the Right to Choose*. New York: Cambridge University Press, 2002.

Jack M. Balkin, ed., *What* Roe v. Wade *Should Have Said*. New York: New York University Press, 2005.

Edwin Black, *War Against the Weak: Eugenics and America's Campaign to Create a Master Race*. New York: Four Walls Eight Windows, 2003.

Marian Faux, Roe v. Wade: *The Untold Story of the Landmark Supreme Court Decision That Made Abortion Legal*. New York: Cooper Square Press, 2001.

David J. Garrow, *Liberty and Sexuality: The Right to Privacy and the Making of* Roe v. Wade. Berkeley and Los Angeles: University of California Press, 1998.

Linda Greenhouse, *Becoming Justice Blackmun: Harry Blackmun's Supreme Court Journey*. New York: Times Books, 2005.

N.E.H. Hull and Peter Charles Hoffer, Roe v. Wade: *The Abortion Rights Controversy in American History*. Lawrence: University Press of Kansas, 2001.

John W. Johnson, Griswold v. Connecticut: *Birth Control and the Constitutional Right of Privacy*. Lawrence: University Press of Kansas, 2005.

Wendy Kline, *Building a Better Race: Gender, Sexuality, and Eugenics from the Turn of the Century to the Baby Boom*. Berkeley and Los Angeles: University of California Press, 2001.

Rachel Kranz, *Reproductive Rights and Technology.* New York: Facts On File, 2002.

Deborah R. McFarlane and Kenneth J. Meier, *The Politics of Fertility Control: Family Planning and Abortion Policies in the American States.* New York: Chatham House, 2001.

Roy M. Mersky and Jill Duffy, eds., *A Documentary History of Legal Aspects of Abortion in the United States.* Littleton, CO: Fred B. Rothman, 2000.

Dorothy Roberts, *Killing the Black Body: Race, Reproduction, and the Meaning of Liberty.* New York: Vintage, 1998.

John A. Robertson, *Children of Choice: Freedom and the New Reproductive Technologies.* Princeton, NJ: Princeton University Press, 1996.

William Saletan, *Bearing Right: How Conservatives Won the Abortion War.* Berkeley and Los Angeles: University of California Press, 2003.

Alexander Sanger, *Beyond Choice: Reproductive Freedom in the 21st Century.* New York: Public Affairs, 2004.

Mary Lyndon Shanley, *Making Babies, Making Families: What Matters Most in an Age of Reproductive Technologies, Surrogacy, Adoption, and Same-Sex and Unwed Parents.* Boston: Beacon, 2001.

Rickie Solinger, ed., *Abortion Wars: A Half Century of Struggle, 1950–2000.* Berkeley and Los Angeles: University of California Press, 1998.

Teresa R. Wagner, ed., *Back to the Drawing Board: The Future of the Pro-Life Movement.* South Bend, IN: St. Augustine's, 2003.

Mary Warnock, *Making Babies: Is There a Right to Have Children?* New York: Oxford University Press, 2002.

Periodicals

Raymond J. Adamek, "*Roe*'s Days Are Numbered," *Human Life Review,* Fall 2001.

Hadley Arkes, "'Judicial Usurpation' and the Unraveling of Rights," *Human Life Review,* Fall 2002.

Jennifer Baumgardner, "*Roe* in Rough Waters," *Nation,* February 10, 2003.

Joseph J. Bozzuti, "Judicial Birth Control? The Ninth Circuit's Examination of the Fundamental Right to Procreate in *Gerber v. Hickman,* " *St. John's Law Review,* Summer 2003.

Dorothy Dunbar Bromley, "This Question of Birth Control," *Harper's Monthly,* December 1929.

Brian Caulfield, "Pregnant Pause: Where Do Frozen Embryos Belong?" *Human Life Review,* Summer 2001.

Christian Century, "Lives of the Embryo," June 28, 2005.

Eleanor Cooney, "The Way It Was," *Mother Jones,* September/October 2004.

Edd Doerr, "Women's Lives, Women's Choices, Women's Voices," *Humanist,* July/August 2004.

Economist, "The War That Never Ends—Abortion in America," January 18, 2003.

John Hart Ely, "The Wages of Crying Wolf: A Comment on *Roe v. Wade,*" *Yale Law Journal,* vol. 82, 1973.

Robert P. George and David L. Tubbs, "The Bad Decision That Started It All," *National Review,* July 18, 2005.

Mary Ann Glendon, "Women of *Roe v. Wade,*" *Human Life Review,* Summer 2003.

Rachel Benson Gold, "Lessons from Before *Roe:* Will the Past Be Prologue?" *Guttmacher Report on Public Policy,* March 2003.

Nat Hentoff, "A Pro-Life Atheist Civil Libertarian," *Free Inquiry,* Fall 2001.

Barbara Hewson, "Coercion in Family Planning: Individual Autonomy Is Pitched Against Communal Values," *Conscience,* Winter 2002.

Wendy Kaminer, "Abortion and Autonomy," *American Prospect,* June 5, 2000.

J.H. Landman, "Sterilization—a Pointedly Frank Discussion of a Grave Social Problem," *Current History,* August 1936.

Paul A. Lombardo, "Facing Carrie Buck," *Hastings Center Report,* March/April 2003.

Mary Meehan, "ACLU v. Unborn Children," *Human Life Review,* Spring 2001.

Newsweek, "The Abortion Revolution," February 5, 1973.

Herbert L. Packer and Ralph J. Gampbell, "Therapeutic Abortion: A Problem in Law and Medicine," *Stanford Law Review,* May 1959.

Rachel Perkins et al., "They Should Not Breed: Feminism, Disability, and Reproductive Rights," *Off Our Backs,* November/December 2002.

Ramesh Ponnuru, "Abortion Now: Thirty Years After *Roe,* a Daunting Landscape," *National Review,* January 27, 2003.

William Saletan, "Unbecoming Justice Blackmun," *Legal Affairs,* May/June 2005.

Gary Thomas, *"Roe v. McCorvey," Christianity Today,* January 12, 1998.

Philip Thompson, "Silent Protest: A Catholic Lawyer Dissents in *Buck v. Bell," Catholic Lawyer,* Spring 2004.

Time, "A Stunning Approval for Abortion," February 5, 1973.

Michael L. Wehmeyer, "Eugenics and Sterilization in the Heartland," *Mental Retardation,* February 2003.

Benjamin Wittes, "Letting Go of *Roe*," *Atlantic Monthly*, January/February 2005.

Web Sites

Health and Reproductive Rights (www.nwlc.org/ display.cfm?section=health). Part of the Web site of the National Women's Law Center, a legal clinic that works through litigation and public education to improve the lives of women, girls, and families, the Web site provides documents and links to articles on contraception, abortion, and other reproductive rights matters.

Lifenews.com (www.lifenews.com). Founded in 1992, Life news.com is an independent news agency that provides news articles and commentary from a pro-life perspective. The Web site contains numerous links and articles about abortion, contraception, and related issues.

Snowflakes Embryo Adoption Program (www.snowflakes.org). Started by Nightlight Christian Adoptions, the Snowflakes Embryo Adoption Program believes that life begins at conception and encourages couples that have undergone fertility treatments to make their unused frozen embryos available for adoption to qualified couples.

Index